Accelerate

A SKILLS-BASED SHORT COURSE

INTERMEDIATE

Series editor: Philip Prowse

PATRICIA LODGE · BETH WRIGHT-WATSON

Heinemann English Language Teaching
A division of Reed Educational and Professional Publishing Limited
Halley Court, Jordan Hill, Oxford OX2 8EJ

OXFORD MADRID FLORENCE ATHENS PRAGUE
SÃO PAULO MEXICO CITY CHICAGO PORTSMOUTH (NH)
TOKYO SINGAPORE KUALA LUMPUR MELBOURNE
AUCKLAND JOHANNESBURG IBADAN GABORONE

ISBN 0 435 28265 4

Text © Patricia Lodge and Beth Wright-Watson 1995
Design and illustration © Heinemann Publishers (Oxford) Ltd 1995

First published 1995

Designed by Portfolio Design Consultancy, Aylesbury
Cover design by Richard Gillingwater
Cover photo by Frank Orel/Tony Stone Images

The publishers would like to thank *Young Telegraph*
for the text on page 62. © The Telegraph plc, London, 1994.

Printed and bound in Great Britain by Thomson Litho Ltd,
East Kilbride, Scotland

96 97 98 99 10 9 8 7 6 5 4 3 2

Contents

Views of language learning

Create two images in your mind: a large oak tree growing in a green field, and a large jigsaw puzzle of a tree which is partly completed.

What has this got to do with language learning? Simply the images of oak and jigsaw represent differing ways of looking at language learning. For many people, learning a language is like doing a jigsaw: the language is broken up into lots of little bits and they are pieced together, one by one, until the whole picture is built up. Incredibly, despite all the discussion over language learning in the last quarter of a century, this is still a popular view and lessons are expected to contain one grammatical point at a time. The bit of grammar is learnt just like that, and the learner goes on to the next bit. Regrettably therefore, most learners leave their English classes with only part of the picture – rather like the partly-done jigsaw you imagined. Leonard Newmark expressed this well nearly thirty years ago in 'How not to interfere with language learning' (*International Journal of American Linguistics*, 32, January 1966):

'If the task of learning to speak English were additive and linear [...] the child learner would be old before he [*sic*] could say a single appropriate thing and the adult learner would be dead.'

The other view compares language learning to the oak. It is natural, growing and changing. An oak is still an oak whether it is the mighty tree you may have imagined or a tiny sapling. All trees are unique, yet share similar characteristics. In this view of language learning, learners learn by doing, by using the language in contexts that interest them. Different learners will learn different things from the same lesson – in the language classroom there is no one-to-one correspondence between learning and teaching, or as David Nunan put it at IATEFL in 1994, 'Why Don't Learners Learn What Teachers Teach?'. The differences between the two approaches are summarized by Dave Willis in *The Lexical Syllabus* (Collins, 1990):

'Form-focused approaches see language as a system of patterns or structures [...] Task-based approaches see language as a system of meanings.'

What's in *Accelerate*?

The oak and jigsaw also help us with the problem of what to include in a book or course. When a jigsaw is complete nothing can be added to it. An oak is never complete – it grows and changes throughout its life. The fallacy of completeness encourages learners to believe that if they ingest the textbook lesson-by-lesson, they will have swallowed the whole of the English language. Nothing could be further from the truth. Any course, any book, can only offer a sample of English. We can expect this sample to be interesting, and generative, in that it will encourage further language learning, but we cannot expect it to be a piece of the jigsaw, which, when fitted together, gives the whole language picture. The four levels of *Accelerate* are not intended to be done one after the other: they are suited to short course students at four different levels. They enable students to grow and develop at their own pace, acknowledging that learning English is something that continues and is not confined to the classroom.

We favour learning by doing. The approach in *Accelerate* is skills based, starting with language use about motivating topics. While each lesson focuses on language form appropriate to the level, that language form is there because the learners need it to carry out the activities and process the texts. Texts and activities are not devised in order to contextualize a pre-specified language syllabus. The language syllabus comes from the texts and activities themselves.

Using *Accelerate*

In creating these materials our aim has been to produce lessons that work: lessons that are transparent to the teacher and student. Each lesson takes a double-page spread, with a clear language focus and skills-summary box. Practice pages for each lesson give vital reinforcement of language focus points and help those learners who like to do extra work on their own. Flexibility is the keynote of *Accelerate*. The Student's Book provides the core, with its combination of lessons and practice pages; the Teacher's Book contains extra ideas for warmers and extension activities, enabling each teacher to tailor the materials to his or her class needs. The clarity and simplicity of the materials cuts teacher preparation time to a minimum and enables the teacher to concentrate on what he or she is best at – relating to and interacting with the students.

For some groups and teachers it will be appropriate to work through the lesson material step-by-step, and then look at the practice pages in class. For others, particularly mixed ability groups, the teacher may wish to refer to the practice pages before, or during, an activity to clarify a language point. Where time is very short, practice pages can be done out of class and the suggested homework omitted. Where there is more time, doing the practice pages in class gives the teacher an opportunity to pay attention to individuals and do some remedial work. Most of the homework activities can also become classwork, if necessary, and we find that starting or ending a lesson by returning homework from a previous lesson is a valuable way of reviewing, particularly when students are able to read, compare and discuss each other's work. The homework is usually suitable for classroom display and will very quickly give an identity to the group and the room.

Most importantly *Accelerate* focuses on the learner: on his or her interests, experience, and ambitions. The great strength of starting from language skills rather than form is that the materials address the learner as a mature human-being. The learner is seen as someone with a lot to offer who may not speak a lot of English, rather than as someone to be addressed as if they were a child because they do not know much English. The word *accelerate* carries with it the idea of speed. These materials do not offer the possibility of covering the same familiar ground in some magically faster way. However they do enable learners to go faster by extending and revising their command of the language through activities that involve them as people.

Accelerate does not cover the whole of English grammar or the whole of the English language. What it does offer are a number of exciting windows into English, and opportunities for learners to climb through those windows and make English their own.

Map of the book

The theme of this unit is experiences of learning languages and approaches to learning them, while focusing on self-help activities.

Lesson 1 *Helping yourself*

Aims: to share language learning experiences and to discuss strategies for learning languages.

Language focus

1 Question forms: *Yes/No* questions
Have you seen a film in English?

2 Questions with *what, how,* and *which*
How often did you speak English last week?
Which English pop singers do you like?

3 Subject questions; *who* and *what* as subject and object
Who's been studying English the longest in your group?

Skills focus

● **Listening** to monologues to get specific information
● **Speaking:** fluency; playing a game and responding to instructions given during the game
● **Writing** an informal letter stating aims for the course

Vocabulary focus

● **Games:** *dice, counters, squares, miss a turn, places*
● **Learning languages:** *bilingual, vocabulary, word map*

Warmer

This is the first lesson, therefore you may need to get to know the students' names. This activity is more fun if students stand on chairs (see below) but you can ask them to stand in a line if you do not think that it is appropriate.
Put chairs in a semi-circle. Ask each student to stand on one of the chairs. Tell students that one end of the semi-circle is A (first letter of the alphabet) and the other end is Z.
Ask students to put themselves into alphabetical order according to their first names, without touching the floor. Students say their names from A to Z and then back the other way.

Or

Jumble three of the questions from the game, and write on the board:
do English learning like you ?
been times England how ? you many have to
the in group who's longest studying your English been ?
Ask students to raise their hands when they have finished.
Mark the stress and intonation in the first question and practise it in chorus:
Do you like learning English?

Ask students to do the same with the other questions. Chorus drill the questions with the class.
You may want to do a revision of question forms here. If so refer students to practice page 66. Look at the Language Summary and students do Exercise 1 individually.

1

Ask students to work in groups of four and give each group a dice and four counters. (Students can make their own counters with coloured card.)

Instructions for the game:

1 One student in each group throws the dice, moves the given number of squares and answers the question from that square.
2 Encourage the students to say as much as they can and tell the listeners to ask questions.
3 Set a time limit of 20–30 minutes. Stop all groups. The student in each group who is nearest to the finish is the winner.
4 Ask the winner in each group to report about one square.
5 You may want to turn to practice page 66 and introduce question forms here as the students have just been using them.

2

If there has been plenty of discussion during the game keep this short and do it as a whole class activity.

3

Ask each group to choose a secretary to write the list. Groups exchange lists and compare them.

Answers

There are no right or wrong answers here. Here are some suggestions:
I remember words by making lists, writing a translation, putting words into sentences, grouping words under headings.
I watch films in English and listen to pop songs.
I read English magazines.
I write to an English pen friend.
I go on exchange visits.

4

🔊 Play the cassette through once. Ask students to work in their groups and tick the ideas. Ask the group with the most ticks to report back to the class.

Answers

This will depend on what students' lists contain. See Activity 5 for all the ideas on the cassette.

5

Ask students to study the word map in pairs. Explain that this type of map is a useful way of recording information and/or vocabulary. They will use them at other times in the course. Indicate the gaps in the map before the class listen to the cassette again and ask students to try to fill the gaps from what they remember from the first listening.

Play the cassette through again. Students work alone to fill in the gaps. Get them to compare their answers in pairs. If necessary play the cassette again, stopping at any answers that have proved difficult.

Answers

1 *lists*	2 *magazines*	3 *books*	4 *songs*
5 *radio*	6 *films*	7 *television*	8 *satellite*
9 *clients*	10 *record*		

6

Ask the students to work alone to choose three ideas from the word map.

Give the class two minutes to move around the room and ask as many other students as they can about their choices and the reasons for them.

For feedback ask students to stand in a semi-circle and get reports from several of them about their findings.

Homework

Prepare for this by explaining the homework while students are still in the circle for Activity 6. Tell them that their letters will be a chance for them to tell you about their individual wants and needs. You may like to ask them to include other information such as language learning background and good things happening to them at the moment.

If you have the time you could tell them that you will reply to their letters. This could be a standard reply with a personal part at the beginning.

Ask students to write about 100 words.

Extend the activity by asking students to keep a note/diary of how they have carried out the ideas from this lesson, ready for another letter later in the term.

Practice *page 66*

Language Summary

Refer students to the game in the first lesson. Get them to find an example of a yes/no question, or refer to the jumbled question in the Warmer: Do you like learning English? Give the statement: I like learning English.

Elicit/revise which auxiliary (helping) words we use for making questions and when we use them, eg when we use the verb *to be*.

Revise the *what/how/which* questions and subject/object questions in the same way.

1

Ask students to complete Exercise 1 alone and compare their answers with a partner.

Extend the practice by asking students in pairs to make up more *who/what/how* questions and give them to another group to answer.

Answers

3 *S*	4 *O*	5 *S*	6 *S*	7 *O*
8 *S*	9 *O*			

2

Ask students to work alone to answer the questions. They then write three more questions about the text to ask another student.

Answers

2 *How many films can you watch in Harlow?*
3 *Where is the Odeon?*
4 *When can I see 'TWELVE-TWENTY' at the weekend?*
5 *What happens to Jim in 'One Wild Night'?*
6 *Who's in 'Miller's Crossing'?*

3

Ask students to complete the sentences in pairs. They should then try to explain why any of the other possible answers are not correct.

Answers

2 *In the evening Premi watches satellite TV.*
3 *When Osmantan visits London he goes to exhibitions to look at the paintings.*
4 *He's listening to English radio.*
5 *When Osmantan visits London he finds it difficult to sleep because he can hear the traffic all night.*

Lesson 2 *Traveller's tales*

Aims: to decide which vocabulary is useful to know when you visit another country and to find ways of learning new words.

Language focus

1 Order of adjectives
It was a **large**, **square**, **blue**, nylon suitcase.

2 Verbs which only take one form: the *-ing* form or the infinitive
I **managed to remember** the vocabulary for cars.
We **practised repeating** new words.

Skills focus

- **Listening** intensively to a monologue to complete a text
- **Speaking:** fluency – exchanging information about holidays
- **Writing** ideas for an advice sheet

Vocabulary focus

- Airport: *arrivals, check-in, departure lounge, duty free, tickets, lost property*
- Luggage: *hand luggage, holdall, rucksack*
- Aeroplane: *captain, flight attendant, in-flight film*

Review

Think of three questions such as:
What colour is your car? (black)
Where did you go on holiday last year? (France)
How many children have you got? (four)
Do not tell the students the questions.
Write the (given) answers only to the questions on the board. .
Ask students to guess the questions that go with the answers by calling out *yes/no* questions only.

Warmer

Tell students about a happy holiday you have had. Include the month and year. Ask students questions about the holiday. Write the month, year and a few words of explanation (eg, camping in Italy).
Ask each student to write (on separate pieces of paper) about three different holidays or countries they have visited. They should use the same form as you did.
Put the students into groups of five. They mix the papers together and make a pile. Ask one student from each group to take the top paper from the pile. The student who wrote it has to tell the group about the place/holiday. The others find out as much as they can about it by asking questions.
Students carry on taking it in turns to take a paper.
Get feedback about one holiday from each group.

1

Ask students to raise their hands if they have visited any other countries. Divide the class into groups of three or four for the discussion, making sure that each group has at least one person who has visited another country. Remind the other members of the group that they must ask questions.
For feedback, ask groups to report back on the countries visited and any language problems.

2

Ask students to work in the same groups of three or four. Get each group to elect a secretary to write the list.
Groups compare their lists and choose a single phrase from the two lists. They should justify their choice.
Write the phrases on the board.

3

Ask students to stay in their groups to talk about Indonesia.
Get feedback by asking each group one of the questions.

Answers

Indonesia: in south-east Asia, consists of more than 13, 600 islands, 1,919,443 km^2.
Tropical climate (average temperature 27° C);
December– March is rainy season, April– November is dry season.
Food: fish, chicken, beef; cooked with a lot of spices, coconut milk, sweet and sour sauces and soups, curry.

4

Activities 4 and 5 link the subject of travelling to a new country and learning new vocabulary. Ask students to think about English and any other languages they have learned.
Play the cassette through once. Ask students to work in their original groups to tick their lists.
Find which group has the most ticks.

Answers

The words and phrases that Beth needed are: what to say in shops, language for meeting people, the answer to 'Are you married?', fruits and vegetables, numbers, words to describe her lost suitcase and clothes, words about cars.

5

Play the cassette again. Tell students to answer questions 1–4 only. They work alone. They then compare answers in pairs. Next focus on the dictation. Ask students to try to fill in the gaps in the text before listening again.
Extend the activity by playing the cassette again and asking students to mark the stress. They then practise speaking at the same time as the voice on the cassette.

Answers

1 *Beth's suitcase was lost and she had to go to the lost property.*
2 *She needed words to describe the luggage. 'It was a large, square, blue nylon suitcase and inside it were my new brightly-coloured cotton clothes.'*
3 *The brakes failed.*
4 *She had to use the words and repeat what had happened many times.*

Dictation

I think out of all the words I learnt before travelling to Indonesia, the numbers were the most useful because I used them all the time right from the first day. But the words I remembered easiest were how to describe things, my suitcase in particular, and how to talk about cars. I think it's when you're forced to use new words that you really remember them.

6

Before looking at the exercise ask students what they mean when they say that they 'know' a word. This should include spelling, pronunciation, collocation (when two items are used together frequently, eg a loud noise, badly dressed, the lion roared) etc.
Ask students to do this alone, checking first that they understand all the methods mentioned.
Then, in pairs students compare their lists.
Feedback: elicit students' ideas, and find the most popular methods.

7

Remind students of the word map in Lesson 1 of this unit. Ask students to work in pairs to complete this map.
To make feedback and checking easier, get one pair to do their map on the board. You can use that as the example.

Answers

aeroplane: *captain, flight attendant, in-flight film*
airport: *check-in, customs, departure lounge, duty free, lost property, tickets*
luggage: *hand luggage, holdall, rucksack*

8

Prepare students by referring back to travel problems raised in Exercise 1 and on the cassette (Beth's problems). Also relate any experiences of your own.
In pairs, students write their tips on large sheets of paper.
Post the papers round the classroom and have a vote for the best.
Extend the activity by asking students to go round to look at the lists again and correct mistakes. Give guidance by suggesting they look for spelling and grammar mistakes.
Return sheets to writers to rewrite a corrected version.

Homework

Prepare this by looking at the word map in Activity 7.
Ask students to suggest possible topics.

Practice *page 67*

Language Summary 1

Look at the example. Make sure students are aware of where to put commas, that is, after each adjective except the one before the noun, eg small, brown, leather gloves.

1

Ask students to complete the table in pairs. To make feedback efficient get one pair to do the table on the board.
Extend the activity by getting pairs to write sentences describing objects, for example, clothes in the classroom.

Answers

opinion	size	shape	colour	material
horrible	large	round	black	cotton
pretty	long	square	green	fur
ugly	tiny	triangular		leather
useful				paper
				plastic
				woollen

2

Ask students to do this exercise alone. Check that the punctuation is correct.

Answers

2 *Small, brown, leather gloves.*
3 *A pretty, small, round, black mirror.*
4 *A small, rectangular, green, woollen bag.*

3

Prepare for this by getting students to describe orally different types of jacket. Emphasise that they should use the words from Exercise 1 on practice page 67 to enlarge their descriptions. For example:
There was a small, black and white, plastic student card.
They should also try to add adjectives of their own.

Language Summary 2

Give students a list of verbs from Lesson 2 Activity 4, the listening exercise: decide, manage, try, practise, want, force.
Play the cassette through and ask students to listen for the words and phrases that follow these verbs. Discuss how they fit in with the explanation in Language Summary 2.

4

Ask students to complete the letter alone and then compare their answers with a partner.

Answers

2 *to improve* 3 *speaking* 4 *to have* 5 *to help* 6 *smoking*
7 *to take* 8 *to move* 9 *studying* 10 *eating*

Lesson 3 *Lots of languages*

Aims: to study a multi-lingual family and to discuss the advantages and disadvantages of learning lots of languages.

Language focus

used to and *would* for past habits and states
My mother **used to** visit us for three months every year.
My parents **would** insist on speaking English at home.

Skills focus

- **Reading** for the main idea and specific information; guessing the meaning of unknown words from context
- **Speaking:** exchanging information and using it to answer questions
- **Listening** for specific information
- **Writing:** a guidance list giving advice

Vocabulary focus

- Colloquial: *pick up, freak, switch, kids*
- General vocabulary: *tantrum, obnoxious, mastered*
- Countries/languages/nationalities: *Germany/German, England/English, Spain/Spanish, Japan/Japanese, France/French, Italy/Italian, Greece/Greek, Turkey/Turkish, Denmark/Danish, Hungary/Hungarian, Czech Republic/Czech*

Review

Vocabulary competition:

Form the members of the class into teams of six or seven students. Give each team a large sheet of paper and ask them to put it on the wall. Ask one student from each group to stay beside their paper and give them a pen. Ask the rest to move three metres away.

Then call out a vocabulary area from the last two lessons (luggage, airports, aeroplanes, countries, useful phrases, etc). The student with the pen writes as many words as they can. Other members of the team may help by calling out words and spellings. They must not go near the board.

After a few minutes call 'All change!' The writer from each team returns to the line and a new member of each team comes to the board. You may keep the same vocabulary area or give a new one.

Repeat the activity until everyone has had a turn at writing up vocabulary.

Give marks for correct words, spelled correctly. Practise pronunciation, check for meaning and any specific collocations. Use the opportunity to extend the vocabulary area.

Warmer

In pairs ask students to tell each other about their family rules. For example, practise a musical instrument every day, only watch a set amount of TV every day, visit their grandparents every week, have sweets only once a week. Give examples from your own childhood.
Several pairs report back to the class.

1

Prepare students by telling them how you feel about some of these questions. Also point out that the length of time you go for will probably make a difference to your behaviour.
Give them time to think quietly about their opinions and then compare with another student. Then ask pairs to form fours and compare opinions again.
Several groups report back to the class.

2

🔲 Play the cassette through once. Ask students to work alone, noting the answers. Play the cassette again stopping to elicit the answers.

Answers

Name	Marie Young
Age now	*45*
Place of birth	*Czech Republic*
Nationality	*Czech*
Husband's nationality	*English*
Number of children	*2*
Children's ages now	*20, 21*
Present home	*Paris, France*

3/4/5

The next three activities are linked because they involve a jigsaw reading.
Give the following instructions to the class and write them on the board. This is especially useful if it is the first time the class has done a jigsaw reading.
Read your text and match each paragraph with its heading.
Read your text again and do Activity 4.
Read and answer the questions for your text only.
Check your answers with someone who has read the same text as you.
Now divide the class and give half Marie's text and the other half Klara's. Give a time limit of 20–25 minutes.
Pair a student who has read Text A with one who has read Text B. Ask them to answer the remaining questions in Activity 5 together.
Identify A and B students and ask students to give you answers to the text they have not read.

Answers 3

Marie	Klara
2 *Marie's decision*	**2** *Learning Czech*
3 *Marie's method*	**3** *Changing from one language to another*

4 *Advice from Marie*
5 *Speaking English in France*
6 *The result*

4 *Problems*
5 *Languages for money*
6 *Learning Spanish*
7 *The future*

Answers 4

Marie

1 *pick up* 2 *bilingual* 3 *switch* 4 *kept it up* 5 *freaks*

Klara

1 *obnoxious*
2 *it would always come back*
3 *have tantrums*
4 *motivated me*
5 *progress little by little*

Answers 5

1 *Three.*
2 *Czech.*
3 *She would speak in one language and then repeat the same sentence in the other language. After a month she would change the order.*
4 *Children should always know which language they should speak to specific adults.*
5 *They went to England when they were young and their parents spoke English to them in the home.*
6 *French. She did not like to feel different with her French friends.*
7 *She had the three languages separately in her mind, like three different worlds.*
8 *From Spanish children on holiday, and later at school.*
9 *She wants to learn another language such as Japanese and to teach any children she might have lots of languages.*

6

Ask students to discuss their advice in groups.
Extend the activity by getting students to write tips, as in the previous lesson, for people living in their country who are married to someone from another country.

Homework

Tell students that they will need information from both texts in the next lesson therefore it is important that they read the other text and complete the vocabulary activity.

Practice *page 68*

Language Summary

Refer students to the Language Summary and the use of *would* when talking about past habits.

1

Ask students to do Exercise 1 alone and check it with a partner. The focus of this exercise is that students choose the correct verb to go with *would* or *used to*.

Answers

2 *used to hate*
4 *used to/would visit*
6 *used to go*

3 *used to/would have*
5 *used to/would speak*

2

This exercise gives more practice of the language point. Ask students to do it in pairs. Encourage them to discuss why they use each item.

Answers

When I was little I used to live in a small cottage in a village. I *would* play with the girl who lived in the house next door. She was French so she *would* speak French to her family, but we *would* speak English together because I didn't speak French. We *would* ride our bicycles everywhere together, but she used to have a better bicycle than me and I was always jealous of her. When I was seven, my family moved into the town, and I *would* only see my friend about once a month. After a couple of years we grew apart; she *would* spend more time with other friends, and so *would* I. Now we live in the same town, but I don't see her much at all, even though I can speak French now!

3

Ask students to work in pairs to do this. They may need the help of a grammar book.

Answers

3 *Gabriella told me that she was going on holiday next week*
4 *The policeman told me that he couldn't help.*
6 'I'm not coming back,' *David said angrily.*
9 *The customer told him that the soup was cold.*
10 'Why didn't you tell me this before?' *Manuel complained.*

4

Students may need a dictionary to do this. Tell them that you want the adjective for each person.
You could have a group competition to see which group can find three more countries, languages and adjectives.
Extend the activity by showing students how stress is marked in dictionaries. Get them to work with a partner to mark stress on the words in the chart, eg: J**a**pan, Japan**ese**

Answers

Country	Language	Person (adjective)
England	*English*	*English*
Spain	*Spanish*	*Spanish*
Japan	*Japanese*	*Japanese*
France	*French*	*French*
Italy	*Italian*	*Italian*
Germany	*German*	*German*
Turkey	*Turkish*	*Turk/Turkish*
Denmark	*Danish*	*Dane/Danish*
Hungary	*Hungarian*	*Hungarian*
The Czech Republic	*Czech*	*Czech*

The theme of this unit is work. It focuses on job suitability and people's prejudices about who should do certain jobs.

Lesson 1 *The right job*

Aims: to talk about personal qualities needed for jobs and to follow a flow chart to find the right job.

Language focus

1 Adjective formation from nouns
Would you describe yourself as **confident**?

2 Using the *-ing* form and infinitive with verbs of preference
I **love to work** closely with others.
Would you like to spend a lot of time in the company of animals?
You **like being** alone.

Skills focus

- **Listening** and taking notes
- **Reading** a flow chart in detail
- **Writing:** taking notes in order to write a paragraph about someone's reaction to the findings of the flow chart

Vocabulary focus

- Adjectives to describe personality: *careful, dynamic, extrovert, friendly, hard-working, imaginative, lively, logical, patient, responsible, smooth-talking, sympathetic, tolerant*
- Jobs: *accountant, disc jockey, environmentalist, nurse, tourist guide, travelling salesperson*

Review

This follows up the homework task from the previous lesson, which was to read one of the texts from Unit 1 Lesson 3.
Demonstrate the task yourself, by speaking for one minute on a chosen subject, eg your family, your best friend.
Ask students to work in pairs; one to talk about Marie for one minute and the other to talk about Klara for one minute.
Students take it in turns to speak. The listeners have to report three pieces of information to the class.

Warmer

Use jobs from Activities 2 and 5. Choose the jobs that students are likely to know in English.
Demonstrate. Put the name of a job on a student's back. The student asks questions to find out what the job is.
Write the names of jobs on sticky labels and put them on everyone's backs. Students mingle to ask questions and find what their job is. If there is a problem about moving around this can be done in pairs or small groups.

While students are doing the activity, collect any errors they make, especially with question forms.
Form a circle. Ask students about their job, eg what do they think are the hours of work, qualifications needed, qualities important for the job, etc.
As a revision of question forms from the previous unit correct any errors you collected with the whole class.

1

Play the cassette through once. Students work in pairs to compare their answers.

Answers

1 *She started to help a friend who was teaching the Vietnamese boat people. She was asked to teach them and then realised that she needed to train as a teacher – which she did.*
2 *It is important to know yourself so that you do not choose a job that does not match your abilities and personality.*
3 *She has many characteristics that are useful for teaching: she is friendly, patient, lively, hard-working. Also there is variety in teaching and this stops her from getting bored.*

This could be a suitable moment to focus on the grammar point: *-ing* form and infinitive with verbs of preference, as it is relevant for this exercise and the ones that follow. Refer students to practice page 69 Language Summary 2, and let them do Exercise 3.

2

Students may need dictionaries to check the meaning of some adjectives.
Ask questions to make sure that students understand the meaning of the adjectives before they listen again.

Answers

friendly, patient, lively, dynamic, hard-working

3

Ask students to work in pairs to match the adjectives with the jobs. Tell them that they need to give reasons for their choices.
Feedback: Write the jobs on the board, elicit the students' choices for each one and write them on the board.

Answers

There are no right or wrong answers to this, as long as students can give reasons.

4

Encourage students to think carefully about adjectives to describe themselves and the job/jobs they would like to do. Include students who already have jobs by asking them to consider the advantages and disadvantages of their present jobs and what they would do if they could change.
Ask students to write down their decisions to keep for later in the lesson. You may like them to name their papers and collect them in.

5

Before reading the chart, pick out vocabulary that may be difficult and pre-teach it. For example: initiative, unsupervised, stamina, orderly, desperate, favours, a good eye for something. Ask students to help each other with the meanings.
Explain how to follow the flow chart by doing the first few questions yourself. For example: *I don't need to be in the company of others more than five days a week.*
Therefore follow the NO arrow and colour (red for NO).
Give students time to work alone and follow the chart.

6

Draw the symbols from the chart on separate sheets of paper. Put them round the walls.
Ask the students to stand by their symbol from the chart. Tell them to take their textbook with them.
Ask students to read the three sentences, a, b and c beside their symbol. This tells them which jobs are suitable for them. Give students time to study the vocabulary, making sure each group has a dictionary.
Put students into pairs. Give them these headings: qualities, jobs, agree/disagree?
Students work in pairs and find out about each other.

7

Refer back to Activity 4 when students recorded their qualities and preferred jobs. Find out how their ideas compared with the decisions of the flow chart.

Homework

The feedback from the previous exercise can be used as preparation for the homework. Ask students to write about what their interviewee said and also whether they agreed or disagreed with the findings of the flow chart.

Practice *page 69*

Language Summary 1

Refer students to Language Summary 1, focusing on the endings of the adjectives. Elicit other adjectives with similar endings.

1

Refer students to the texts in Unit 2, Lesson 1. Ask them to find the adjectives.

Answers

liveliness – lively	sympathy – sympathetic
confidence – confident	competition – competitive
efficiency – efficient	logic – logical
optimism – optimistic	imagination – imaginative
ambition – ambitious	

2

Ask students to do this exercise alone. They then compare answers with a partner.
To extend the activity get pairs to write two more sentences using words from the box in Exercise 1.
Or
Ask pairs to write six or more sentences using adjectives from the texts. Tell them to write them with gaps and give to another pair to complete.

Answers

2 optimistic	3 sympathetic	4 confident	
5 ambitious	6 imaginative	7 competitive	8 logical

Language Summary 2

Elicit examples of students' likes and dislikes.
Play the cassette through again. Students work alone noting examples of the *-ing* form and the infinitive.

3

Ask students to do Exercise 3 alone, then write three sentences about themselves.
Write topic areas on the board: food, travel, school, homework, television, sport, cinema. Ask students to make questions, eg
What do you prefer, flying or travelling by sea?
Do you like eating sweet things? etc.
Tell students they have two minutes to ask their questions of as many people as they can.

Answers

2 to work	3 to get	4 travelling, to have
5 working, to earn	6 working, being, to find	

4

Refer the students to the examples and ask them to break their first names into syllables. Show the students how syllables are marked in dictionaries.
Extension 1: To revise the stress exercise from practice page 68 Exercise 4, ask students to mark the stress on the words in Exercise 4. Practise saying the words with the students.

Answers

two syllables	three syllables	four syllables
florist	ac**count**ant	in**ter**preter
jockey	**barr**ister	pho**tog**rapher
lawyer	beau**ti**cian	so**lic**itor
plumber	**cash**ier	
poet	**ed**itor	
	pharmacist	
	sur**vey**or	

Extension 2: Ask students to number the syllables and mark the stress on the adjectives in Exercise 1 on practice page 69.

Lesson 2 *Can you judge by appearances?*

Aim: to discover commonly held views about people's appearances.

Language focus

1 Present perfect simple and present perfect continuous
I**'ve lived** here all my life.
I**'ve been** working with a charity for a long time.

2 *for* and *since*
I've been farming **for** three years, **since** Dad asked me to help him.

Skills focus

● **Reading** short texts from a magazine to find specific information, and finding the meaning of words in context
● **Listening** for specific information
● **Writing** questions based on one of the texts
● **Speaking:** asking and answering questions about a text

Vocabulary focus

● Jobs: *barrister, cashier, doctor, editor, farmer, hairdresser, optician, secretary, train driver, undertaker*
● Words from the texts: *gob-smacked, wellies, domesticated, paperwork, a high-rise flat*

Review

Play Hangman to revise adjectives from the previous lesson.

Warmer

Groups make a word map around the word job.
Or
Before students open their books give them a list of jobs from Exercise 1. Ask students to work in pairs to discuss the personal characteristics (good and bad) that they would expect to find in people doing these jobs.

1

Ask students to make their first choice alone and then compare answers with another student, giving reasons. Get one pair to write their answers on the board in two columns headed Men and Women. Use this as a basis for feedback. Find out if everyone agrees with this pair.

Answers

There are no right or wrong answers because anybody can do any job, as the lesson will show. However the students' likely answers will probably be:
Men: *barrister, farmer, hairdresser, train driver, undertaker, doctor, optician*
Women: *barrister, hairdresser, secretary, cashier, doctor, optician*

2

Explain to students that there is a pause on the cassette between the answers to questions 5 and 6 and that question 6 refers to what is going to happen in the next activity.
▣ Play the cassette through once.
Ask students to compare their answers and discuss whether they believe that they personally judge people by their appearance and whether people in general make such judgements.
Play the cassette again if necessary.

Answers

1 *A television reporter.*
2 *The Prime Minister.*
3 *In a two-seater plane.*
4 *She thought that the pilot had not turned up.*
5 *She assumed that the pilot would be a man.*
6 *Students have to do the next exercise to find out if they make judgements according to people's appearance.*

3

Ask the students to decide alone which jobs the women do. Write the letters of the photographs of the six women on separate sheets of paper. Do this twice. Divide the class into two groups. Give each group a set of papers and get them to pass them round until every student has written a job on each piece of paper. Collate the answers by asking students from each group to count up the results and write them on the board. Give the correct answers and see how many correct guesses there were. Find the student with the most correct answers. Then elicit the reasons that they had for their choices.

Answers

Picture a: *the barrister* **Picture d:** *the doctor*
Picture b: *the sales assistant* **Picture e:** *the train driver*
Picture c: *the farmer* **Picture f:** *the hairdresser*

4

Ask all students to read about the doctor. Introduce the idea of scanning a text to get specific pieces of information. This means that students do not need to understand every word, only enough to find·the information asked for.

Answers

1 *false* 2 *true* 3 *true*
4 *false: She used to be a bus driver.*
5 *false: She would like to live with people who have children, but she doesn't want any of her own.*

5

Make this into a competition which will encourage the use of scanning techniques as these increase reading speed.
Ask students to raise their hand as soon as they have answered all the questions.
Get feedback immediately from the first student to finish.

Answers

1 *The doctor.*	2 *The farmer.*
3 *The train driver.*	4 *The barrister.*
5 *The hairdresser.*	6 *The hairdresser's.*
7 *The farmer.*	8 *The sales assistant's.*
9 *The sales assistant.*	

6

Ask students to work in groups of four to try and understand the vocabulary without using a dictionary.
Do the first one with the whole class.

Answers

1 – *b (It means very surprised, in fact so surprised that you are lost for words.)*
2 – *a (Wellies is an abbreviation for Wellington boots, which are rubber boots worn for farming, gardening and walking.)*
3 *a*   4 *c*   5 *b*

This would be an appropriate place to introduce both the Language Summaries on practice page 70. They have relevance for Activity 7.

7

Ask students to choose a text or give them out yourself. Move round correcting question forms. You may need to follow up with remedial work on question forms.
Give a time limit for writing questions (five to eight minutes) so that all the questions are exchanged at the same time.

Homework

Prepare students by putting them into groups (or working with the whole class) to write questions for the interview.
Elicit some questions from the class first, eg:
What is your job?   *What do you have to do?*
Why did you choose it?   *How long have you been doing it?*
What qualities do you think are necessary for the job?
Have you got those qualities? etc.
Talk about paragraphing. Remind students that each paragraph covers one topic only.

Practice *page 70*

Language Summary 1

Ask students questions about the texts in the lesson which will produce answers using the present perfect simple and continuous. For example:
How long has the hairdresser been doing her job?
She's been doing her job for over 20 years.
Refer students to the Language Summary and ask them to find more examples from the texts.

1

Ask students to work in pairs, one doing the paragraph about Richard while the other does the one about Alex.
Ask students to take it in turns to read out their exercise to their partner. Ask the listener to stop if they feel there has been a mistake.

Answers

Richard

2 *has worked*	3 *has already done*
4 *has been working*	5 *has not done*
6 *has been living/has lived*	

Alex

7 *has been learning*	8 *has not passed*
9 *has cut*	10 *has gained*
11 *has been coming*	12 *has applied*
13 *has not been*	

Language Summary 2

Ask students to find examples of the use of *for* and *since* in the text. We often use *for* and *since* with the present perfect to say how long something has continued.
We use *for* + a length of time   We use *since* + starting point
Use the lesson time as an example:
When did this lesson start? How long have we been in this lesson?
It started at . . . We've been here since . . . We've been here for . . .
   How long have we been in this class?
   For half an hour.
SINCE 9.00

9.00 a.m.	NOW	10.00
Lesson started	9.30 am	Lesson ends

2

Ask students to work alone on Exercise 2 and compare their answers with a partner.
Ask students to work in pairs to tell each other about themselves and then write the sentences down.

Answers

since	for
1988	a long time
I came to England	ages
I was about sixteen	four days
the beginning of the lesson	nearly eight months
my last birthday	over twenty years
	the last few days
	three years

Lesson 3 *Career counsellors*

Aims: to give and receive advice about choosing a job, through interviews between clients and counsellors.

Language focus

Modal verbs of obligation and advice
You **have to** have a university degree.
You **must be** good at dealing with people.
You **should** apply in writing.
You **needn't** have a specific qualification.
You **don't have to** have a teaching qualification.

Skills focus

- **Listening** to an interview for the main idea and for specific information
- **Speaking:** a roleplay between counsellor and client
- **Writing:** filling in an information sheet

Vocabulary focus

- Work: *counsellor, client, qualifications, recommendations*

Review

Display the homework round the walls.
Ask students to look at each other's work. From the jobs mentioned, they choose the job that they would most like to do and the job they would not like to do.
Get them to tell a partner. Ask two or three students to report back to the class.

Warmer

1 Choose six professions.
2 Find six pictures of unknown people, one for each job you have chosen. Cut pictures from magazines.
3 Do not tell the students how you have matched them.
4 Students work in groups of four to give a job to each person. They must be able to give reasons for their choice.
5 Tell them your answers and reasons.

1

Ask the students to imagine David's character and job from his appearance. Write the ideas on the board to check later.
Before listening, elicit:
– ways of getting advice about careers,
– what happens when you go to a counsellor.
Establish that counsellors only recommend, they do not dictate to their clients.
▭ Play the cassette through. Then refer back to the students' guesses (on the board) to see if anybody was right.

Answer

David is doing part-time work in a library.

2 and 3

▭ Depending on the ability of the class you could either get everyone to listen to the cassette and fill in the information card, or divide the class. Ask one half to fill in the card and the other half to write down the questions that the counsellor asks. The students form pairs, with one person from each group. Get the students with the questions to ask their partners for the answers from the information card.

Answers 2

Age:	*25*
Qualifications:	*'A' levels, a degree in geography*
Personality:	*good with people, patient, practical*
Previous jobs:	*postman, porter in a hospital*
Present job:	*part-time library work*
Job preferences:	*work outside, travel, use French*
Recommendations:	*environmental work*

For the answers to Exercise 3, please refer to the Tapescript. If necessary practise sentence stress and question intonation. This would be an appropriate place to introduce the Language Summary on practice page 71 as the students will need to use the language practised (modals of obligation and advice) in the next exercise of this lesson.
Refer students to the Language Summary and ask them to do Exercises 1 and 2.

4

Preparation for roleplay:
Give a time limit for the preparation (five to ten minutes). Students should prepare in two groups: clients and counsellors.

Clients:

Remind them of the warmer where they matched jobs with the people in photographs. Tell them that they are one of the people in the photographs on page 17. Make sure that they know they must pretend to be this person. The clients fill in the information cards alone.

Counsellors:

Ask students to work in groups to prepare their questions. They can use the questions from David's interview and add to them to find as much information as they can. Remind them that they will need to be flexible because each client will have different needs.

Roleplay:

Take care with classroom management and instructions. Tell the counsellors to sit in a circle facing outwards. Each client faces a counsellor. If you have a large class and this would be difficult, your students will have to work in pairs in their places, and then either move places, or work with the student behind them or next to them on the other side. You may need to allow longer for the first interview because the students will need to relax into the activity. Arrange a signal so that everyone will stop talking at the same time. After approximately three to five minutes ask the clients to move round two places clockwise and start a new interview. The counsellors do not move.

5

Debriefing:

Ask students to form two groups, counsellors and clients. Get counsellors to discuss:
– easy clients
– difficult clients
– what advice they gave and why.
Get clients to compare the advice they were given and decide which was the most suitable.
Feedback: Ask two or three counsellors and two or three clients to report back to the whole class, summarising the main points of their discussions.
Follow up error correction. While students are doing the roleplay collect errors under these headings:
– grammar, focusing on modals
– vocabulary
– pronunciation
– register, appropriacy
Write the errors on the board and invite corrections from the class. Indicate the corrections by using a red pen or chalk. If there have been a lot of pronunciation errors, write the words on the board and encourage students to use dictionaries to find the stress. If a lot of students are having problems with a specific sound you may want to demonstrate it.
Extend the practice by getting students to repeat a shortened version of the roleplay. This time they should think about what was said in the error correction. Finally, reverse the roles.

Homework

Prepare this by getting students to suggest the name of a famous person and giving information about their personality and career.
Fill in the information on the board, in the form of an information card.
To extend the activity, ask students to use the information cards they have done for homework to make a poster about their famous person.

Practice *page 71*

Language Summary

Elicit the language the counsellor used to tell David what qualifications he needed for jobs and how she gave him advice.

🔊 You may want to play the cassette again.

1

Ask students to do Exercise 1 with a partner.
Follow this by asking them to take it in turns to tell their partner the advice they gave or received in the roleplay.

Answers

1	*mustn't be*	2	*needn't wear*
3	*mustn't smoke*	4	*should take*
5	*must speak*	6	*should ask*
7	*needn't phone*		

2

This gives more practice with modals.
Ask students to work together to discuss their opinions and then to write sentences. Get pairs to compare their answers with another pair.
Several students report back to the class so as to get an example for each job.

Answers

All the answers will be different. Here are some possible answers:

2 *hotel receptionist: must be good at dealing with people, but he or she doesn't have to have special qualifications. A hotel receptionist must be patient and should be able to work alone.*

3 *nurse: must have special qualifications and should be able to work as part of a team. He or she has to be in good health and should be patient and accurate.*

4 *florist: has to be imaginative and also should be practical. A florist must be good with their hands but needn't have special qualifications.*

5 *salesperson: must be good at persuading people to buy things. A salesperson needn't be creative but should be good at dealing with people.*

3

Before looking at the example formal letter of application, elicit the layout of a formal letter and put it on the board. This should include suitable greetings and endings.
Study the letter in Exercise 3 together with the class and compare it with the version on the board.
You may want to give half the class one advert and the other half the second advert.
Ask students to work in pairs to write the letter. Monitor for mistakes.
Put all the letters for the florists on one side of the class and those for the overseas sales managers on the other.
Students who wrote for the florists should correct the sales managers' letters and vice versa. Allow five minutes for correction and also look for mistakes yourself. Remind the class of the importance of neatness and presentation.
Ask each group to decide which letter from each group would warrant an interview.

The theme of this unit is description; in particular fashion developments, houses and objects.

Lesson 1 *The future of fashion*

Aim: to discuss the advantages and disadvantages of new developments in clothing.

Language focus

Defining relative clauses
  a coat **that changes colour with the weather**
  Massimo Osti is the man **who has brought these fabrics to the shops.**

Skills focus

- **Reading** a headline to predict what is in a newspaper article and reading for specific information
- **Listening** for information to complete a table
- **Writing** an article about new fashion ideas
- **Speaking:** discussion about the advantages and disadvantages of following fashion

Vocabulary focus

- Clothes: *a sweatshirt with logo, tights, ski-wear, thermal underwear, cycling shorts, jackets, blouse, T-shirt, shirt*
- From the text: *fibre, odour-free, fabric, temperature-sensitive, synthetic, fragrance*
- Designs: *stripes, patterns*

Review

This revises modal verbs of obligation and advice using the homework from the previous lesson.
Ask students to work in groups of four.
They take it in turns to speak, using the information from the cards they filled in for homework. They should include what the person needed to do to be successful and give advice for the future.

Warmer

Ask students to work in pairs to tell each other about any new clothes that they have bought in the last two months. Ask them to make a list of everything they bought, and say if each item was cheap or expensive.
Put pairs together to form groups of four and ask them to compare their findings.
Groups report back so that you can find the people who buy the most clothes.
Note: Treat this as a light hearted piece of fun, but be sensitive if there are big differences in income among your students. Leave out the pricing part.

1

Ask students to work with a partner to do the matching. Check the answers and ask them to discuss the questions. Ask around the class to see if everyone likes the same clothes.

Answers

2 *a*	**3** *b*	**4** *c*	**5** *f*	**6** *e*

2

Tell the students to work with a partner to discuss the headline without looking at the passage, and to choose a meaning for it. Get feedback quickly and write their ideas on the board. Ask students to read the article quickly to see if they chose the correct sentence. Explain that we skim a text to get the general idea of what it is about, so we do not have to read and understand every word. To encourage this do not allow students to spend too much time reading the passage.

Answer

Clothes that change colour.

3

The next three activities develop more intensive reading skills. Ask the students to work alone to match the headings and then to compare their answers with a partner.

Answers

1 *6*	**2** *4*	**3** *3*	**4** *2*	**5** *5*	**6** *1*

4 and 5

Ask students to read the text again. If they are finding the vocabulary difficult tell them to do Activity 5 first. They may need to use dictionaries. Ask students to work in pairs.

Answers 4

Clothes that change colour: coat, jackets, golf sweaters, ski-wear
Patterns that disappear: shirt stripes, logo on sweatshirt
Protection from mosquitoes: tights

Answers 5

1 *d*	**2** *e*	**3** *c*	**4** *b*	**5** *f*	**6** *a*

6

Before playing the cassette, ask students to work in pairs to describe the pictures to each other.
▭ Play the cassette through and ask students to work alone to answer the questions. Then they compare their answers with a partner.
Play the cassette again only if there have been problems of understanding.

Answers

1 *dolphin*   **2** *flowers*   **3** *discos*

7

Before playing the cassette again ask students to work in pairs to try to complete the table.

▣ Play the cassette through and ask students to work together to complete the table. They should note their correct answers from their first attempt.

Answers

Advantages	Disadvantages
attracts people's attention	*embarrassing parts may change*
pretty designs	*colours*
good to have something really	*washing these clothes sometimes*
different to wear	*causes the original colours to*
can be an advantage to draw	*change*
attention to some parts of	
your body	

8

Prepare students by finding out who has bought clothes recently, who buys clothes for them, and whether they buy clothes for other people.

Ask students to work in groups of four to discuss the questions. Monitor for errors.

Get feedback from each group. Ask for a show of hands to answer the question about fashion-consciousness.

Homework

Prepare students by brainstorming ideas for each of the three headings. Write the ideas on the board.

Practice *page 72*

Language Summary

Refer students to the Language Summary. Point out that no comma is needed before *who, where* and *which* in a defining relative clause.

Ask students to find examples in the text on page 18.

1

Ask students to do Exercise 1 with a partner.

Answers

2 *I'm going to take the shoes that squeak when I walk back to the shop.*
3 *This is a very unusual T-shirt that glows at night.*
4 *These new fibres that Massimo Osti invented are brilliant.*
5 *Golfers who need warm clothes are now wearing temperature-sensitive clothes.*
6 *These tights that are impregnated with fragrance are a new design.*

2

After they finish this exercise ask students to make similar sentences defining jobs and places. For example:
A teacher is a person who . . .   A library is a place where . . .

Answers

2 *who* 3 *–* 4 *–* 5 *which/that* 6 *which/that*

3

Ask students to work in pairs to label the pictures.
Extend the activity by asking them to make a word map with the heading of *clothes*.

Answers

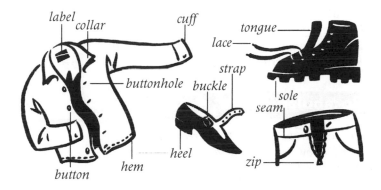

4

This exercise gives more practice in formal letter writing, following on from the letter in Unit 2 Lesson 3 (practice page 71) replying to a job advertisement.

Ask students to work alone to match the numbers with the area of the letter.

Extend the activity by brainstorming things that go wrong and that people complain about. Write the ideas on the board and ask students to choose one to write a letter of complaint about.

Answers

From top to bottom: *2, 6, 5, 8, 4, 1, 3, 7*

Lesson 2 *Homes*

Aims: to learn about an unusual house and to describe a room and its contents.

Language focus

1 Open conditionals
If you **can't** go up, **go** down!

2 Participle adjectives
Quarmby was very **interested**.
I found the work very **interesting**.

Skills focus

- **Speaking:** taking part in an information gap activity
- **Listening** in order to label a diagram
- **Reading** a newspaper article for specific information
- **Writing** a description of a room

Vocabulary focus

- Homes: *caravan, bungalow, terrace, detached, mansion, castle, nest, burrow, tent, semi-detached, flat, apartment, studio, bedsit*
- Rooms: *bedroom, bathroom, study, dining room, garage, kitchen, day room, living room, en suite bathroom*
- Shapes: *square, circular, rectangle, oval, ovoid, curved, circle*

Review

This revises the vocabulary of clothes.
Ask the class to walk round the room while you play some music. When the music stops they have to find a partner and stand back to back. They take it in turns to describe what their partner is wearing.
Repeat this three or four times.

Warmer

Ask students to work in pairs to take it in turns to describe their homes.
One or two pairs report back to the class and lead into Activity 1 by focusing on how many different types of houses there are.

1

Ask students to work in groups of three and to elect a secretary. Stick to the one-minute rule and get feedback from the group with the longest list. You may like to check whether any of the groups with shorter lists have house types not on the longest list.

2

Let students look at the pictures. Then ask them what they think it would be like to live underground.
Ask students to answer the questions alone and to compare their answers with a partner.

Answers

1 *He wasn't allowed to build it above ground because the land is in beautiful countryside.*
2 *No. Arthur Quarmby, Britain's leading expert on 'earth shelters', has one.*
3 *Damp; you still have to keep to building regulations; lighting; what to do with the soil from the hole where the house is.*
4 *Because you don't have outside walls you can spend more money on the inside.*
5 *He obviously loves it, he found the work very interesting and he is afraid of heights so particularly liked working underground.*

3

Before playing the cassette check that students understand *observatory*. Also point out the swimming pool as the blue area opposite the main entrance, and the side entrance at the round end of the egg, opposite the observatory.
▭ Play the cassette through once and ask students to work alone to label the rooms.
Ask students to compare their answers with a partner. Only play the cassette again if there have been problems.

Answers

In the middle of the house: *day room*
Clockwise from the observatory: *dining room, kitchen with the garage leading off it, (entrance), study, bedroom with en suite bathroom, (side entrance), bathroom, guest bedroom, third bedroom, swimming pool, living room*

4

This would be an appropriate place to introduce practice page 73, Language Summary 1. The language is relevant for the next three activities.
Keep this brief. Ask students to work in pairs. Make sure they give at least two reasons for and against. Two or three pairs report back to the class.

5

This would be an appropriate place to introduce Exercise 4 on practice page 73. It is directly relevant to the information gap exercise in Activities 5 and 6.

Check that students know the names of the four shapes, which are: a rectangle, a square, a circle and an ovoid.

Prepare students by choosing one of the shapes yourself and describing your dream room, giving reasons for your choices. Ask students to draw their room on a large sheet of paper. Tell them to think about how they are going to describe everything to their partner. Give a time limit for this preparation (five minutes).

Tell students that they do not have to be artists. If they really find drawing difficult they could write the names of the items or suggest symbols for furniture which you can agree before the activity.

6

If possible students should work with a partner who they do not sit near. They should make an effort not to look at each other's drawings.

Students take it in turns to describe their room.

When you see that most pairs are nearly finished, warn the class that you will stop the activity soon.

Ask students to check their drawings and say why they had chosen their items.

Then repeat the process with new partners.

Monitor for error, particularly for problems with prepositions of place and phrases such as top right, half way down, which help with the information gap activity.

Display the plans round the room: the original with the copy. Let students mingle to look at them, and see how the two drawings compare. Ask them to talk to each other to find out more about the items in the rooms.

Homework

Prepare students for this either by telling them briefly about your ideas for a dream house or by brainstorming ideas. Put a few notes and ideas on the board. Remind students to refer back to Activities 2 and 3 for ideas and ways of describing them.

Practice *page 73*

Language Summary

Refer students to Language Summary 1. Ask them to find examples of an open conditional in the text about Stuart Bexon.

1

Ask students to do this exercise alone. Check the answers round the class.

Answers

2 *ask*	**3** *Don't expect*	**4** *don't need*
5 *can spend*	**6** *Consult*	**7** *might consider*
8 *can't get*		

2

This gives more practice with open conditionals. Ask students to work together to write the sentences.

Answers

2 *If he finds a nice location Stuart Bexon will build a second home for himself.*

3 *He can invite architects from other countries to see his house if they have (the) time to come.*

4 *He might build a second part to his house if he gets approval from the local council.*

5 *If he has enough money Stuart Bexon may buy the field next to his house.*

3

Students often make mistakes with the use of *-ed* and *-ing* adjectives, which are common particularly to express opinions. Therefore an understanding of the rules behind them will help students to recognise further examples.

Ask students to do the exercise alone and compare their answers with a partner.

Answers

2 *interesting* **3** *surprised* **4** *tiring* **5** *satisfying* **6** *bored*

Follow the exercise with speaking practice.

Ask students to talk to a partner to discuss what they think of horror films/the latest fashions/modern architecture/this book/programmes on television.

4

Ask students to do this exercise alone. Then check the answers round the class.

Answers

The triangle is inside the circle which is on the cylinder. Next to the cylinder is the cube which is also under the rectangle. The octagon is around all the other shapes.

Lesson 3 *Advertising and selling things*

Aims: to describe objects orally and in writing.

Language focus

Intensifiers
very large country house
£450 is much **too** expensive.
It's small **enough** to fit in your bag.

Skills focus

- **Listening** to someone trying to sell something, and listening for specific information
- **Writing** descriptions of objects to make an advertisement
- **Speaking:** a roleplay – selling something
- **Reading** for specific information

Vocabulary focus

- Describing a computer: *size, age, type, condition, secondhand, brand new, nearly new, micro, medium size, lap top, personal, as new, perfect, excellent, good, broken, bad, light pen, twin drives, bargain*
- Houses: *quiet location, walled garden, village, double garage, unfurnished, reception rooms, conservatory, accommodation*
- Clothes: *high quality, unbleached, shrinkage, heavyweight cotton, rugby shirt*

Review

Read out several Dream Room paragraphs from the homework. Students try to guess who they belong to.

Or

Display the paragraphs and any drawings on the noticeboard.

Warmer

You may like to use Activity 1 as the warmer, as this introduces the theme of the lesson – describing things.

Or

Choose an object, animal or person, and tell the students which of these categories it belongs to. They have to guess what it is by asking *yes/no* questions only. The student who guesses the object chooses the next thing to be guessed.

1

Ask students to work in pairs to discuss the riddle. Keep to the three-minute time limit.

Answer

a roll of transparent sticky tape, such as sellotape

Give pairs five minutes to write another riddle. Pairs then swap riddles and try to solve each other's.
Read one or two out to the class.

2

Ask students to work alone to match the descriptions with the pictures. They then compare their answers in pairs.

Answers

1 *f*	2 *e*	3 *c*	4 *d*	5 *a*	6 *b*

3

Before they read remind students that they do not need to understand all the vocabulary or read every word carefully. Introduce the idea of scanning the text for information. Students may need to use a dictionary for the abbreviations although encourage them to try to deduce meanings from the context.
Ask students to work with a partner to discuss their answers.

Answers

1. *The whale ceramic wall plaque.*
2. *The very large country house in Widdington.*
3. *From all major retailers.*
4. *Medium and extra large.*
5. *condition, including, per calendar month, reference, central heating*

4

Students are by now familiar with word maps. Ask them to study this one and see if they can add anything.
Ask students to work in pairs to create a word map. Tell them to use a large sheet of paper.
Ask pairs who have drawn word maps for the same articles to compare their maps.
Display the maps on the wall so that students can share the vocabulary.

5

Before playing the cassette through check that students understand the vocabulary in the table.
▭ Play the cassette and ask students to compare their answers.

Answers

features in the advertisement	true	false	correct description
nearly new		✓	quite old
4 months old		✓	about 4 years old
excellent condition		✓	damaged by falling off desk
twin drives	✓		
light pen working perfectly		✓	doesn't work properly
bargain		✓	£450 too expensive

6

Refer students to the Language Summary on practice page 74. Exercises 1, 2 and 3 are directly related to the following activities of the lesson.

Prepare students for the roleplay by eliciting phrases Lesley used on the cassette. For example: *How old did you say it was? So it's not really in 'excellent condition' like you said in the advert, is it?* Focus on the tone of voice that Lesley and the seller use.

▣ Possibly drill the relevant phrases from the cassette. You may like to play the cassette through again.

Suggest that students might like to 'sell' the item that they used for their word map.

When pairs have decided on their item allow a short time for planning.

Monitor for error during the activity. Focus on expressions used and the intonation.

7

Brainstorm the information needed for one of the objects and write the ideas on the board.

Ask students to work in pairs to make their lists for the other objects.

One pair for each object read their list to the class.

Possible answers

Hi-fi: *age, condition, brand, technical specifications, price*
Armchair: *age, condition, colour, size, brand, comfort, price*
Shirt: *age, condition, colour, size, brand, price*
Television: *age, condition, brand, technical specifications, colour or not, price*

8

Give each group a large sheet of paper and encourage them to use coloured pens to design the advert. If this is not possible, they will have to write neat, short, clear descriptions that persuade people to buy.

Remind students that adverts are to encourage people to buy things.

Display the adverts. Have a class vote to find the most persuasive one.

Homework

Elicit what goes to make a good advert: clear layout, eye-catching, relevant information but short and to the point, truthful.

Practice *page 74*

1

Refer students to Language Summary 1. Exercises 1, 2 and 3 are directly related to the activities and texts in Lesson 3.

Answers

2 *too*   3 *very*   4 *very, too*   5 *very*

2

This exercise also gives practice with the structure.

Answers

2 *small enough*   3 *too big*
4 *too expensive*   5 *quickly enough*
6 *early enough*

3

This exercise also gives practice using *too much* and *too many*, which are used on the cassette.

Answers

2 *enough*   3 *enough*   4 *too many*   5 *too much*
6 *enough*   7 *too many, enough*

4

This gives more practice with word maps and builds on the vocabulary met in this unit. Make sure that students understand that the words are divided into verbs and nouns before they start it. Some words, such as lamp, switch, could go in several rooms.

Answers

Living room – *nouns: switch, lamp, armchair, fireplace, sofa, rug, coffee table, lamp*
verbs: watch TV, relax, snooze, entertain
Dining room – *nouns: cutlery*
verbs: eat, dine, entertain
Kitchen – *nouns: oven, switch, cupboard, freezer, cutlery, cooker*
verbs: prepare, grill, boil, bake, chop
Bedroom – *nouns: chest of drawers, bedspread, blanket, duvet, wardrobe, lamp*
verbs: sleep, snooze, snore, dream
Bathroom – *nouns: basin, bath, shower, toilet, switch*
verbs: shower, go to the toilet, shave

The theme of this unit is unusual games and sports and the dangers involved. Students design their own game.

Lesson 1 *New Sports*

Aims: to find out about more unusual sports and to design an advertisement for a sport.

Language focus

Modals of deduction
They **could** be soldiers.

Skills focus

- **Listening** to a conversation to complete a table about three people's favourite sports
- **Writing:** designing an advertisement and taking notes in preparation for writing a paragraph
- **Speaking:** speculating about what people are doing and exchanging opinions and information about sports

Vocabulary focus

- Sports: *abseiling, bungee jumping, gliding, parachuting, rock climbing, squash, underwater tennis, white water rafting, paintball*
- Equipment: *belt, flag, mask, goggles, armband, gas canisters, holster, ropes, ball, racquet*
- Associated words: *equipment, training, skill, rules*

Review

Put the adverts from the homework for Unit 3 Lesson 3 on the wall as a display.

Warmer

Find a picture of someone taking part in a sport and show it to students for a few seconds. Turn it over quickly, then show it to them again for a few seconds. Gradually allow students to see more of the picture until they can describe it fully.

1

Use the Language Summary and Exercises 1 and 2 on practice page 75 to introduce the topic of sport and practise the target language. Ask students to do Exercise 1 alone and check the answers with the whole class. Ask students to work in pairs to do Exercise 2 and compare their deductions with another pair. Correct any errors involving modals. The work in these exercises leads to the speaking activity in Lesson 1 Activity 1. Ask students to work in pairs to speculate about the photograph. Encourage them to use the target language. Finally each pair reads a sentence to the class. They should use

phrases given in the target language.
Find out if anyone has played paintball. If so ask them to tell you about it.

Answers

1 *They could be soldiers. They are playing a game called paintball.*
2 *They are holding guns which do not fire bullets but paint.*
3 *So that they do not get any paint in their eyes.*
4 *It is a game for two teams whose aim is to capture a flag. They do this by having a mock battle and eliminating each other by firing paint. Marshals referee the game and watch for safety.*

2

Ask students to work in pairs to help each other with the vocabulary. After a while, let them use dictionaries. Ask students to mark the stress on the words using their dictionaries.
Get pairs to describe the picture using the vocabulary.

3

Ask students to work in pairs to do the matching exercise and discussion. Do the first one with the class to illustrate that you want them to use modals of deduction.

Answers

1 *b, e, h*

4

▭ Play the cassette through once to find out who plays which sport.

Answers

1 *Carl: bungee jumping*
2 *Shaun: paintball*
3 *Karen: underwater tennis*

5

▭ In their groups each student chooses whose information they are going to record. Play the cassette again and get students to share the information about their person with the other group members.

Answers

For the answers please refer to the Tapescript.

6

Before starting the discussion, give students some ideas to consider by asking if they think it is a good idea to pretend to kill each other as in paintball. Think about the part that aggression plays in sport. How important is winning, etc? Get the students to talk in their groups and then join another group to pool ideas.

7

Ask students to complete the advertisement in their groups.

Remind students of the advertisements they created in the Unit 3 Lesson 3 homework and the ingredients that go to make a good advertisement. For example, what are the designers trying to achieve?

Answers

£15	4p	guns	gas	20	safety

8

Give each group an A3 size piece of paper or card. Give a time limit, eg eight to ten minutes, so that everyone finishes together. Warn groups of the time passing.

9 and Homework

Before starting the interviews make it clear that the game/sport should be one the students know about although they don't have to play it. Give students time to note their ideas under each heading. Ask students to work in pairs and take it in turns to interview each other. Explain the homework so that students realise that they need to take notes on the interview. Feedback from interviews: ask two or three students to give details of the person they interviewed. To extend the activity, ask students to prepare short presentations about a game or sport. The presentations should be delivered in groups or in front of the whole class. Give the class something to listen for during the presentation, such as information or errors, comments on structure. Afterwards correct errors, including work on planning, where needed.

Practice *page 75*

Language Summary

Refer students to the language used in Lesson 1 Activities 1 and 2 and look at the Language Summary.

1

Ask students to do Exercise 1 alone and to compare answers in pairs.

Answers

3 *Jan can't play basketball because he's too short.*
4 *Miguel must have liked the paintball game because he's going again next week.*
5 *Carolina must have played squash before because she's got her own squash racquet.*
6 *Vasilli and Francesca can't be at the swimming pool because I've just seen them playing tennis.*
7 *Ali and Azim can't have been to the new leisure centre yet because they don't know where it is.*
8 *Emma must have got her new trainers because we're going running together this evening.*

2

This activity gives freer practice with modals. Do one example with the whole class, then ask students to work in pairs. Ask the pairs to show their ideas to another pair and choose the best one to read to the class. Monitor for the correct use of modals.

It is not important whether the information is correct for the game or not, as long as deductions have been made. However, here are some details:

1 Lacrosse – a game similar to hockey, but the ball is thrown and caught with a netted stick called a crosse.
2 Curling – played on ice with a large round object called a stone. You slide the stone along the ice to try to reach a marked place.
3 Cribbage – a card game played by two, three or four people.
4 This does not have a name – two very long, bendy sticks with nets on the end. You have to pass the ball to each other.

3 and 4

Ask students to do these exercises in pairs and add more sports from the lesson or from their knowledge. Tell them that some of the sports mentioned could be in more than one column.

Answers 3

sports you can practise alone	sports you can play with another player	team sports
aerobics	*boxing*	*American football*
cycling	*cycling (a tandem)*	*basketball*
sailing	*golf*	*cricket*
swimming	*judo*	*cycling**
	sailing	*football*
	squash	*polo*
	table tennis	*rugby*
	tennis	*sailing*
		volleyball

(*if you enter a race with a team of cyclists)

4

This exercise can be done in pairs, groups, or as a competition to see who can get the most correct answers in the shortest time.

Answers

1 *football, polo, American football, basketball, volleyball*
2 *golf*
3 *aerobics*
4 *American football, cycling, sometimes cricket, polo*
5 *squash*
6 *cricket*
7 *usually cricket, sometimes tennis and squash*

Lesson 2 *The price of fun*

Aims: to read and talk about the dangers of becoming addicted to or obsessed by games.

Language focus

1 Position of adverbs of frequency
Sometimes I do the odd night in the pub.
I **never** play the fruit machines.

2 Present simple for habits and routines.
I **come** here almost every day.
I never **play** the fruit machines.
I usually **come** here after school.

Skills focus

- **Listening** to four people talking together, in order to fill in a table
- **Reading** a newspaper article for specific information
- **Speaking:** exchanging opinions

Vocabulary focus

- Arcade games: *video games, fruit machines, amusement arcades, to gamble*
- Money: *coins, notes, cash, grant, fees, savings account*
- Obsessions: *an addict, an addiction, to feed a habit, to cure someone*

Review

Revision of modal verbs of logical deduction. Ask a student to choose a famous person. The rest of the class guess who it is by asking a maximum of ten *yes/no* questions.
Remind students how to draw conclusions as they discuss who the person might be. For example:
He can't be from South America; we know he isn't from Europe, or the Middle East.

Warmer

Tell students about an occasion when you or someone you know won something. Brainstorm situations where it is possible to win something, eg raffles, races – horse, running, dog – , competitions in magazines, raffles, lotteries, bingo, fruit machines, game shows on TV.
Ask students in pairs or groups to tell each other about when they or anyone they know has won a prize. Ask them to say how they felt, what they won, etc.

1

Ask students to work in pairs to do the activity. Ask one pair to write their words on the board so that their list forms the basis of the feedback. Make sure other pairs do not just copy from

the board! Focus on the meaning and pronunciation of any problematic words.

Answers

The picture shows an amusement arcade with games machines. The place is probably noisy, bright, crowded (or empty), possibly dirty.

The people may be happy, sad, excited, frightened, angry, rich, poor, optimistic, pessimistic, lucky, unlucky, etc.
You and the students can use your imagination or experience to describe your own feelings.

2

This is vocabulary preparation before listening to the cassette and reading the text. Ask students to work in pairs to help each other before using a dictionary. Check their understanding of the words before moving on.

Answers

1 *c*   2 *d*   3 *g*   4 *b*   5 *a*   6 *e*   7 *f*

3

▭ Play the cassette through once and ask students to fill in the table alone. Ask them to compare answers in pairs.
If necessary play the cassette again. Stop at specific places if students found some answers difficult.

Answers

1 **Philip**
25
pretty often
he's bored, wants to try his luck
he works for himself as a graphic designer

2 **Jane**
16
almost every day
finds video games fun
does a paper round after school, some from her mother

3 **Paul**
17
once a week or every two weeks
thinks video games are quite good
a Saturday job

4 **Alistair**
19
a couple of times a week if he's bored
to relax and escape from study and exams
his grant, works in a pub, helps on a market stall

This would be a suitable time to introduce Language Summary 1 on practice page 76. Exercise 2 could be used as a diagnosis to find out how accurate the students are, and students could then do Exercise 1 as a follow up to any remedial teaching.

4

Either tell students to cover the article or write the headline on the board and ask students to close their books. They then spend a short time thinking about the two questions.
One or two students tell the class their ideas. Then ask students to skim the article and discuss the accuracy of their predictions with their partner.

5

The students should be able to decide on the correct summary without reading the article again. Allow re-reading only if they are having problems. If they do, remind them to skim because they do not need to understand every word to be able to do the task.

Answer

2

6

Give students time to read the article carefully and answer the questions, although they still do not need to understand every word.
To extend this activity, ask students to work alone and underline three more words that they do not understand. They then work in pairs to try to guess the meanings from context and only use the dictionary if they cannot guess.

Answers

1 *raiding a building society, stealing mother's jewellery, removing money from savings account, stealing, shoplifting, selling own things and taking other people's things and selling them*
2 *the atmosphere with the flashing lights; because they want to; because of problems at home or school or with relationships*
3 *Because the games are played alone.*
4 *By carrying out an information campaign and by giving informal counselling and holding sessions where young people can talk about the problem in groups.*

7

To prepare students for the discussion elicit one good thing and one bad thing about fruit machines. Ask for reasons for each opinion.
Tell students that they must decide one way or the other and be able to give reasons.
Ask students to work in groups of four. Ask each group to elect a spokesperson to report back to the class.
After feedback the class votes with a show of hands to see how many individuals agree with the statement.
Extend the activity by using the ideas from the discussion to plan a 'for and against' essay. Ask students to write it for homework.

Homework

Prepare students by looking at the structure of the letter on practice page 76 Exercise 3.
Elicit the structure for a letter. Then ask students to match each heading with the letter on practice page 76.
They should include: type of greeting, introductory sentence, reason for writing (in this case advice), closing sentence, greeting at the end.

Practice *page 76*

Language Summary 1

▭ Play the cassette again and ask students to write the adverbs of frequency that they hear and notice their position in the sentences.

1 and 2

Ask students to do these alone. Then check the answers with the whole class.

Answers 1

1 *I sometimes go to the arcade. Sometimes I go to the arcade.*
2 *Miguel never plays the fruit machines.*
3 *Alice plays video games every day. Every day Alice plays video games.*
4 *Catharine has been to this arcade many times.*
5 *Joelle has often been to several arcades in one day. Often Joelle has been to several arcades in one day.*
6 *Blake seldom spends more than £10 a week in the arcade.*
7 *Amy is always at the same video game every evening. Every evening Amy is always at the same video game.*
8 *I must always know how much money to limit myself before I start playing.*
9 *You can occasionally find Joe by the fruit machine on the left. Occasionally you can find Joe by the fruit machine on the left.*

Answers 2

1 *The team always arrives late for the match.*
3 *They never play video games.*
4 *Do you often win your matches? Do you win your matches often?*
7 *They are on time every day. Every day they are on time.*
8 *They never spend more than £5.*
10 *I have been to this leisure centre many times.*

3

This will be a revision for students at this level. Ask them to do the exercise alone and then compare their answers with a partner.

Answers

2 *go*	3 *have*	4 *eat*	5 *am*	6 *spend*
7 *train*	8 *travel*	9 *compete*	10 *watch*	11 *do*
12 *comes*	13 *gives*	14 *helps*		

Lesson 3 *Make your own game*

Aim: for students to write their own game.

Language focus

Defining and non-defining relative clauses
  The pair **who** start must throw the dice and move their counter.
  What is the name of the smallest continent in the world, **which** is the home of the Emperor Penguin?

Skills focus

- **Listening:** a dictation conducted by the students themselves, and listening for specific information to answer questions in a quiz
- **Writing** questions for a game

Vocabulary focus

- Playing games: *dice, counter, to move, to have a turn, square, winner, correct, incorrect, shuffle*
- Quiz words: *bone, accommodation, meteorologist, average*

Review

Ask students in groups of four to compare their letters from the homework from Lesson 2. Ask them to focus on the suitability of the advice given, layout, greetings at beginning and end, opening sentence, spelling, grammar.

Warmer

Ask students to work in pairs and write down as many board games as they can think of. For example: Scrabble, Monopoly, Trivial pursuit, snakes and ladders, ludo, Cluedo, chess, draughts.
The pair with the longest list read it to the class.
Note: Students do not need their books for Activity 1. Do not let them open their books so that they do not see the dictation in Activity 3.

1

▣ Play the cassette through. Students will hear the questions twice. Ask students to work alone to try to answer the questions. Then put students into groups of four or five to share their knowledge. Tell each group to elect a secretary to write their group's final answers.

2

Ask the groups to exchange sheets and mark the answers with the whole class. (This avoids cheating!)
Note: It would be nice to give a small prize, such as a sweet each, or a cheap pencil or pen to members of the winning group.

Answers

1 *the ear*
2 *32*
3 *According to the Guinness Book of Records, 'I' is the most common word in spoken English.*
4 *accommodation*
5 *Mount Fuji (in Japan)*
6 *the weather*
7 *English – it is the mother tongue of 350 million people and is used additionally by another 1,150 million people; in all about one third of the world's population.*
8 *women*

3

This activity is an interesting way to introduce rules. It is enjoyable for students and gives practice in speaking clearly, spelling, as well as helping to build the confidence of quiet students. It needs careful classroom management and clear instructions but is always successful.
Tell students that they are going to play a general knowledge game. Explain that they will learn the exact rules from each other.
Instructions for 'Shout dictation':
Put students into pairs, A and B. Tell pairs to sit back to back, if possible separated by at least a metre.
Make sure that students cover the other dictation in their books. Tell A Students that they start by saying the first line to their partner, who should write it down. Tell them they may need to ask for words to be spelt. Elicit the correct question:
How do you spell that?
When B Students have written down what A has dictated, they dictate line 2 to their partner. They take it in turns to dictate and check their answers together when they have finished.
Play background music during the dictation to encourage students to speak loudly and clearly.
When everyone has finished, ask comprehension questions to check understanding, eg:
How many people can play?
Where does it start?
What equipment do you need to play?
You could introduce the Language Summary on practice page 77 here. The language will help students to write the questions correctly.

4

Ask students to work in pairs to compose their questions. They may need reference books, however the questions should not be so obscure that no one can answer them.

Give each pair ten pieces of card or paper. Students will play in groups of eight or ten. Therefore, if possible have four or five different colours of card.

Give a time limit for the question making (ten to fifteen minutes). While students are working on the cards go round helping and monitoring for errors.

Put students into groups of eight or ten. Shuffle the cards and play the game. If necessary demonstrate with one group in front of the class to start with.

Homework

Prepare students by looking at the example in the homework box. Elicit what language is generally used when we give instructions, ie imperatives.

Brainstorm common objects that the students use often. Choose one and elicit the instructions you would expect to find for it.

Practice *page 77*

Language Summary

Write on the board:
The Emperor Penguin has its home in Antarctica. Antarctica is the smallest continent in the world.

Show students how to join the two facts in each sentence using *which*:
The Emperor Penguin has its home in Antarctica, which is the smallest continent in the world.

Then look at how the question about the penguin on the question card in Lesson 3 Activity 3 is formed.

1 and 2

Ask students to do Exercises 1 and 2 in pairs. Check the answers round the class.

Answers 1

3 *Mickey Mouse, who starred in one of the first Disney films, is over 50 years old. ND*
4 *Greece is the country which started the Olympic Games. D*
5 *The elephant is the animal that has the longest memory. D*
6 *The world's largest spider, which has a leg span of 27 cm, lives in South America. ND*
7 *The cat which lived to the greatest age was owned by someone in the south of England. D*

8 *The largest iceberg, which was bigger than the size of Belgium, was seen in the South Pacific in 1956. ND*
9 *Big Bill, who was the heaviest pig ever recorded, weighed over 1,000 kilos. ND*
10 *The most expensive diamond ever, which was sold in 1900, cost $12,760,000. ND*

Answers 2

2 –   3 *that/which*   4 *who*   5 *which*   6 *which*
7 *who/that*

3

Make this into a competition.

Ask students to work in pairs to find the subjects as quickly as they can.

Ask them to raise their hands when they have found all 15. Stop everyone and check the answers.

Extend the activity by asking students to work in pairs to:
– mark the stress on the words,
– write the name of the person who studies each subject and
– mark the stress.

They may need to use dictionaries.

Answers

Each lesson in this unit tells part of a short story about the unusual events that follow a visit to the dentist.

Lesson 1 *A mystery*

Aims: to follow the first part of the story and to give practice in describing feelings.

Language focus

Time linkers
First she got up and walked around.
After that she whistled, and hummed to herself.
He looked up **as** she walked in.

Skills focus

- **Reading** to get the main ideas and details of what happens in the story
- **Speaking:** predicting and telling a story
- **Listening** for specific detail
- **Writing** a description using time linkers

Vocabulary focus

- Adjectives to describe feelings: *angry, annoyed, anxious, calm, relieved, happy, impatient, puzzled, nervous, satisfied, surprised, worried*
- Dentists: *extraction, drill, teeth, surgery, gas cylinder*
- Flying: *fare, float, helicopter, jet plane, refuel*
- Accidents: *mishap, stretcher, rescue*

Review

This activity revises giving instructions.
Describe a scene, giving students time to draw what you say. Get them to compare pictures with each other. Then ask students in turn to give the instructions back to you while you draw on the board.

Or

Check answers to the vocabulary puzzle from practice page 77. If you did not do this during the last lesson, ask students to work in pairs with dictionaries to find the noun for the person who studies each subject.
Tell them to mark the stress for each word, eg:
bi**ol**ogy – bi**ol**ogist
med(i)cine or **med**icine (both ways of pronouncing this word are given in the dictionary) **doc**tor.

1

Use this as a warmer. Ask students to draw or write down two things they are afraid of. Give a time limit of one minute. Ask students to mingle and find any others who are afraid of the same things. Ask students to stand together to tell each other how they feel and why.

2

Ask students to do this activity alone and then compare words with a partner.
Get a show of hands to find students who are not afraid of dentists. Ask those who are for their experiences.
Write the adjectives on the board to check spelling.

3

Students need to understand this vocabulary before they read the story. Ask them to work in pairs. Check their understanding by asking comprehension questions.

Answers

1 *wrinkled = with lines on the face*
2 *fidgeting = moving in an impatient way*
3 *hummed = sang without opening the mouth*
4 *burst out = spoke suddenly*
5 *without further ado = without any more delay*
6 *drummed his fingers = made a noise with the hands to show impatience*

4

Tell students to read the first part of the story alone.
This would be a good time to introduce the language focus of the unit in preparation for students creating their own story.

5

Ask students to cover the rest of the page before doing this exercise so they do not read the next part of the story, which would spoil the prediction activity.
Ask students working in pairs to put the vocabulary under the correct headings. For efficient feedback ask one pair to do the exercise directly onto the board.
Because students will need to use this vocabulary to predict the story, practise pronunciation of the words.

Answers

dentist	flying	accidents
drill	fare	ambulance
extraction	float	mishap
gas cylinder	helicopter	rescue
surgery	jet plane	stretcher
teeth	refuel	helicopter

6

Link this activity to the target language of the lesson. Write the list of linkers from practice page 78 on the board. Tell students to choose three and that they have to use these in their story as well as all the words from Activity 5.

Discuss the structure of a good story: beginning, middle, end. Give a time limit for preparation.

When two pairs are put together, ask each student to tell part of their story. Ask the listening pair to listen for the linkers used and for correct pronunciation of the vocabulary from Activity 5 as well as noting how the story differs from theirs. Finally ask some students for the linkers they heard and some for a synopsis of a story they heard.

7

Ask students to read the text and answer the questions alone.

Answers

1 *Another patient who is in the waiting room and the dentist.*
2 *He has just finished making a phone call and is putting the receiver down.*
3 *The window.*

8

Ask the students to do this in pairs. Get answers from around the class and correct any pronunciation problems.

Answers

The answers may vary, and as long as students can justify them that is all right.

9

▭ Play the cassette through once. Students work in pairs to answer the questions. Play the cassette again if necessary. Ask if any of the students' stories are similar.

Answers

1 *False – she was horrified (cried out in horror).*
2 *False – the nurse was in the room at the time of the incident.*
3 *False – the dentist saw them.*
4 *True.*
5 *False – no one does.*

Homework

Prepare students by doing vocabulary Exercises 3 and 4 from practice page 78. Ask students to use the words from these exercises and from Lesson 1 Activity 8 in their description. Ban the use of certain adjectives that are often overused, such as frightened. Make sure students understand the meaning of nervous as it is used in English.

Ask students to write about 100 to 150 words and remind them to join their ideas with time linkers.

Practice *page 78*

Language Summary

Ask students to work in pairs to underline the linkers in the story from Lesson 1 Activity 4.

They then discuss the function of each linker. Next they check their ideas by studying the Language Summary.

1

Ask students to do Exercise 1 alone.

Answers

2 *Before*   3 *As*   4 *after*   5 *as soon as*

2

Students should do Exercise 2 with a partner.

Answers

While   as   Firstly   then   As soon as   as   while   As soon as

3

Ask students to work in pairs. Check their answers by writing the scale on the board.

Answers

1 *b*   2 *c*   3 *d*   4 *a*

Though native English speakers may have different opinions as to which word in each pair is stronger, those in the B column are probably slightly stronger than those in A.

Answers

terrified – petrified
scared – frightened
nervous – worried
tranquil – calm

4

Do the first sentence as an example to make sure students understand the correct grammar following prepositions. Ask students to complete this alone and then talk to a partner about what they have written. Monitor for correct grammar.

5

Ask students to do this alone and then compare answers.

Answers

2 *impatient* 3 *relieved*   4 *nervous*   5 *calm*
6 *puzzled*   7 *satisfied*   8 *anxious*

Lesson 2 *Adventure*

Aim: to continue the story, focusing on describing sequenced events in the past.

Language focus

Past simple and past continuous
  I **was washing** my hands outside when it **happened**.

Skills focus

* **Reading** for the main idea and to find mistakes in a text
* **Listening** to a story in order to put events into a sequence
* **Speaking:** a roleplay of a telephone conversation
* **Writing** a dialogue

Vocabulary focus

* Revision of vocabulary from Lesson 1: *anxious, patient, calm, mishap, disappearing, embarrassed*
* Informal language: *to be in good shape, to shake your fist at someone, to grab the receiver, to swear, guess who I've been talking to, to burp, a nudist*

Review

Tell students that they have exactly three minutes to write about the story so far. Tell them that you will not look at any mistakes of language but are interested in their descriptions. Put students into pairs to take it in turns to read what they have written to each other.

Or

Collect in the descriptions of the students' visits to the dentist from the Lesson 1 homework. Correct them and display them as a wall newspaper under the headings: *Positive and Negative Memories*.

Warmer

Choose 15 words that you would like to revise from Lesson 1 and write them on the board.
Ask each student to choose five of the words.
Read out a definition of one of the words.
If students think that the definition is correct for one of the five words they have chosen, they cross it off.
The first person to cross off all five words shouts Bingo!

Or

Tell the story so far but include five mistakes.
Students listen and write the mistakes down.

1

You may want to leave this activity out if you use the Bingo warmer. It would be a good warmer especially if extended by asking pairs to choose their own words from Lesson 1 to jumble and pass to another group to sort out.

Answers

1 *anxious*	2 *calm*	3 *embarrassed*
4 *patient*	5 *mishap*	6 *disappearing*

2

The last part of the story from Lesson 1 is included here to revise and to make the sequence of events clearer.
Tell students to cover the text in the left-hand column because they should know it from the previous lesson.
Read the text from the previous lesson aloud and stop several times before some key words and ask students to guess what the next word is going to be. They call it out or write it down. Stopping places might be:
Oh no! Mrs Crisp cried in . . .
Did he jump . . .
Mrs Crisp looked very . . .
. . . in the doorway staring at the . . .
Then ask students to read the rest of the text alone. Make sure they understand that they have to cross out the statements that are not true.
Ask students to do this alone. Check the answers round the class. Then ask students to work in pairs to put the statements that are left into the correct order.

Answers

The false statements are:
2 *False, he floated out.*
5 *False, the window was already open.*
7 *False, she thought it had a strange smell.*

The order of events is 1, 9, 10, 4, 8, 3.

3

This activity practises the past simple and past continuous so this would be a suitable place to introduce the language focus.
Look at the time line in the Language Summary on practice page 79. Students could also do Exercise 1 on the same page.
Note: Do not go on to Exercise 2 because this refers to the next part of the story.
Ask students to work in pairs to decide on the order of the pictures and create a story. Do not tell them if they are correct.
Monitor for mistakes of pronunciation of the vocabulary previously practised in Lesson 1 and for use of past simple and continuous.
🎵 Play the cassette through once. Ask students to work alone noting the order. They then compare their answers in pairs.
Find differences between this story and students' own stories.

Answers

2 *d*　3 *e*　4 *f*　5 *c*　6 *b*

4

Ask students to work alone to find the mistakes in the text. They should raise their hands when they have found them. Stop the activity and check the answers with the class.

Answers

1 *Mr Crisp did not see the helicopter, it was looking for him.*
2 *The weather man said that the wind might blow Mr Crisp towards France. It did not actually happen.*
3 *Mr and Mrs Crisp were not going to France on holiday, but the dentist asked them if they were.*
4 *Mr Crisp made himself burp after he had seen the nudist camp because burping made him lose height.*
5 *He landed on some telephone wires and a farmer took him to a telephone box.*
6 *He did not phone Mrs Crisp. He phoned the dentist.*

5

To prepare students for the roleplay review the dentist's feelings and worries and those of Mrs Crisp. Discuss how we show our feelings with our voices.

If time permits, you may want to put all the students who are Mr Crisp together and all the dentists together to prepare. When the roleplay has begun allow students three or four minutes and then stop everyone.

Ask one pair to demonstrate (a confident pair). Praise them first and then discuss how they could improve content, intonation and correct any language mistakes.

Continue the roleplay.

Finally, if there is time, ask several pairs to perform. Always give the rest of the class something to listen for, eg:
– have all the events of Mr Crisp's adventure been included?
– pronunciation of vocabulary
– which tenses are used?
– can you tell how the dentist and Mr Crisp are feeling?

Homework

Prepare students by getting one pair to write the beginning of their dialogue on the board.

Focus on layout, speech marks, etc. Also refer students to the text in Activity 2.

Practice *page 79*

Language Summary

Look at the time line in the Language Summary.
Ask students to find more examples of the past simple and continuous from the text in Lesson 2 Activity 2.

1

To consolidate, ask students to do Exercise 1 alone and compare the answers in pairs.

Answers

2	*went into*	3	*sang*	4	*was washing*
5	*shouted*	6	*sat down*	7	*opened*
8	*was cleaning*	9	*screamed*	10	*jumped up*
11	*ran out*	12	*heard*	13	*said*
14	*turned round*	15	*was standing*	16	*was watching*

2

Refer students to the Language Summary and ask them to work in pairs.

Answers

2 *The other patients waited patiently while Mrs Crisp was talking to the dentist.*
3 *Mr Crisp saw a nudist camp when he was flying over the south of England.*
4 *The dentist and Mrs Crisp were trying to find Mr Crisp when all the patients went home.*
5 *Mr Crisp shook his fist at the pilot when he was flying past the passenger jet.*

3

Read out three different verbs (eg called, liked, wanted) so the class can hear how each ending is pronounced.

Students work in pairs to group the rest of the words. Tell them that they cannot do this silently, but should try to say the words.

If students are interested look at the rules with them and see if they can work them out.

Answers

/d/ *breathed, cancelled, enjoyed, happened, joined, listened, opened, screamed*
/t/ *helped, jumped*
/ɪd/ *fainted, floated, reported, started*

4

Ask students to work in pairs using a dictionary if necessary.

Answers

actions	equipment	the mouth
drill	*dental floss*	*false teeth*
extract	*(a) drill*	*fillings*
fill	*gas*	*gums*
inject	*needle*	*teeth*
polish	*syringe*	
	toothbrush	
	toothpaste	

Extend the activity by asking students to mark the stress on each word.

They can also tell their partner about their dental experiences so that they practise the words, eg:
I've got a lot of fillings but I've never had any teeth extracted.
Give an example based on your own experiences.

Lesson 3 *Homecoming*

Aims: to finish the story and to report what happened.

Language focus

1 Reported statements
   I told him you were here.
   The dentist told her that her husband would be unconscious
      for a while.

2 Reported questions
   He asked me what the name of the gas was.
   He asked me if you were here.

Skills focus

- **Speaking:** roleplaying an interview
- **Writing** a newspaper report

Vocabulary focus

- Reporting verbs: *to ask, to say, to talk, to shout*
- Feelings: *sympathetically, grimly, cruel, hard, to be worried sick*

Review

This activity revises the pronunciation of *-ed* endings. Give a list of regular past tense verbs from this unit and ask the class to work in pairs to put them under the three headings according to the different ways of pronouncing the final *-ed*: /d/, /t/, /ɪd/.

Warmer

Vocabulary review competition

Divide the students into two or three groups according to the size of the class, with approximately eight in each group.
Ask each group to make a queue facing the board but a couple of metres from it. Get one student from each team to come to the board and give them each a pen or chalk.
Give a vocabulary area such as dentists, accidents, feelings and get each writer to write as many words as they can. Members of their group may help by shouting words, but they must not approach the board.
After a short time change the writers and the vocabulary area.
Check spelling and meaning and find the group with the most correct answers which are not the same as the other group(s).

1

Tell the class that they should not look at their books while they try to remember the story. Encourage them to make notes, though they should use whole sentences when they report back.
Put pairs together to tell each other what they remember. You could also ask groups to retell the story, quickly, round the class.

2

Look at the dictionary definition with the class and elicit occasions when you might feel grim, eg: When you are just about to go into the dentist's to have all your teeth extracted. When you have flu or have had too much to eat or drink.

3

Ask students to read the text quickly and answer the questions alone.
You may want to focus in more detail on the use of language to convey Mrs Crisp's feelings: grinding her teeth angrily, 'He'll wish he was still unconscious,' she muttered grimly.

Answers

1 *To get the name of the gas so that he could start his journey again.*
2 *He gave him the name of the usual gas that dentists use so that he would not be able to fly on.*
3 *Because Mr Crisp did not want to speak to her, he wanted to get away from her, he had caused her a lot of worry and he wasn't worried.*

4

Ask the students to work in pairs to tell the final part of the story. Encourage them to focus on how both Mr and Mrs Crisp were feeling in each picture and the intonation they would use each time they spoke.
One or two pairs report their endings to the class.
▭ Play the cassette through once while the students listen. Ask around the class for the answers. Also, elicit how Mrs Crisp's feelings changed during the extract.
▭ Students may like to listen to the complete story at this point. If they do it will help to remind them of the events and prepare them for the following activity.

5

This activity links directly to the language focus of the lesson. Focus first on reported statements, using Language Summary 1 on practice page 80. Students do Exercises 1 and 2.

Now focus on reported questions. Refer students to Language Summary 2 on practice page 80. Students do Exercise 3.

Make Activity 5 into a chain story.

Tell students to choose an adjective, a past tense verb or a reporting verb from the story so far.

Demonstrate by telling them the word you have chosen and report an event from the story including your word.

Go round the class asking each student to report an event including the word they have chosen.

Help the students to correct their sentences if they make mistakes. This activity is focusing on a language point so accuracy is important.

6

Roleplay

Explain that because what happened to Mr Crisp was so funny, the local newspaper is interested.

The students form groups of four.

Note: If you have an odd number of students leave out one of the characters in one group or have two reporters.

Group A (reporters) work together to prepare questions to ask the three other members of the group. Groups B, C and D work in their groups to prepare the information they want to give for their character.

Encourage students to develop the characters and their feelings. For example, what is the Crisps' marriage like? During the roleplay there will always be two participants who are not being interviewed. Tell them to listen to the current interview, and possibly take notes, because they will need the information for their homework.

Monitor and give feedback on: expression, tenses – past simple/continuous, reported speech.

Homework

Prepare students by getting them to work in their groups to plan the report orally. They will all have to take notes. Remind them to supply a headline for their story.

Practice *page 80*

Language Summary 1

Ask the students to refer to the Language Summary and then to find the reported statements in the text in Lesson 3 Activity 3.

1

They should complete this exercise in pairs.

Answers

2 *She said she hoped he hadn't been waiting too long.*
3 *She told him that he had to have a tooth out.*
4 *She told him that she was going to give him some gas.*
5 *She said that he could now lie back and relax.*
6 *She told him that the gas seemed a bit strange, so she would open the window.*
7 *She said that she was just going to get the dentist.*

2

Students can do this on their own and check their answers in pairs or round the class.

Answers

2 *told*   3 *replied/said*   4 *explained/said*   5 *told*

Language Summary 2

Deal with this in the same way as Language Summary 1, again asking students to find examples of reported questions in the text in Lesson 3 Activity 3.

3

This is further structural practice, and can be done by the students working alone or in pairs.

Answers

2 *Mrs Crisp asked if she could go in next.*
3 *She asked if he had jumped out.*
4 *Mrs Crisp asked the dentist how Mr Crisp could go up.*
5 *The dentist wondered if they were planning a holiday.*

4

Ask students to do the reading task alone. Check the answers quickly.

Look at the layout and talk about who we send postcards to and why we write them. Elicit whether we use formal or informal language.

Extend the activity by getting students to imagine that they have gone on a surprise holiday during term time. Ask them to write postcards to each other telling their friends about the holiday.

Answers

1 *His dentist.*
2 *On the south coast of England.*
3 *The dentist's post code.*
4 *When we want to add something extra to a letter or card.*

The theme of this unit is different types of crime and ways of punishing these crimes.

Lesson 1 *Hidden secrets*

Aims: to give opinions about what kind of prison sentence smugglers should get.

Language focus

The passive
Where **is** the luggage **searched**?
Her baggage was **searched**.
The books **were examined**.
He **won't be prosecuted**.

Skills focus

- **Listening** to a monologue to put information into the correct order
- **Reading** a report in order to complete a text
- **Speaking:** giving opinions about different types of prison sentence
- **Writing** a newspaper article

Vocabulary focus

- Airports: *baggage reclaim, green channel, customs officer, suitcase, luggage, bag*
- Smuggling: *to smuggle, disguise, drugs, cocaine, conceal, drugs baron, heroin, search, sniff, marijuana*
- Police language: *interrogate, prosecute, arrest, convict, prison sentence*

Review

Display the stories (homework from Unit 5 Lesson 3) round the walls and tell students to read them and vote for the best story and also the best headline.

Warmer

Brainstorm the stages of a journey by plane. Then ask students to do Exercise 3 on practice page 81.

1

Ask students to discuss the photograph in pairs. Ask some pairs to report back to the class. Ask if anything has ever happened to them on a journey.

Answers

The photograph shows a uniformed customs officer with a dog sniffing someone's luggage. These dogs are specially trained to sniff for drugs, food and other products banned by customs.

2

If students have done Exercise 3 on practice page 81 during the Warmer, they will probably be familiar with most of the words. If they haven't, ask them to work in pairs and help each other.

Answers

baggage reclaim – where you wait to collect your luggage after your flight. It's usually a conveyor belt
disguise – to alter the appearance of a person or thing so that it will not be recognised
green channel – part of the customs area you go through if you have no items that you need to pay duty on or that are illegal to bring into the country
interrogate – to ask a lot of questions about a crime, often over a long period of time
prosecute – to take a person to court because they are accused of doing something that is against the law
search – to examine someone's body and clothing, looking for eg drugs, weapons, concealed items
smuggle – to bring something into a place or country secretly
sniff – to breathe in (usually loudly and hard) so as to smell something
suspicious – strange or not quite right

3

🔲 Play the cassette through once and ask students to answer the questions alone. They then compare answers with a partner.

Answers

1 *drugs*
2 *specially trained dogs*
3 *in the baggage handling area*

4

The students should try to put the events in order before hearing the cassette again. They should work with a partner.
🔲 Play the cassette through and ask students to check their answers.

Answers

3, 8, 1, 2, 5, 9, 7, 4, 6

5

Check that students understand the meaning of the words in the box. Explain that these are to be used for both texts. Divide the class into A and B groups.
Ask students to read their text and to discuss their answers with a partner from the same group. They may need to use dictionaries.
When they have finished check the answers and get pairs to test each other on their text so that they will know it well enough to tell a student from the other group about it.

Answers

Text A

1	*couriers*	2	*arrested*	3	*X-ray*	4	*quantities*
5	*concealed*	6	*deliver*	7	*convicted*	8	*debts*
9	*parcel*	10	*prison sentence*				

Text B

1	*couriers*	2	*X-ray*	3	*quantities*
4	*parcel*	5	*convicted*	6	*prison sentence*
7	*debts*	8	*deliver*	9	*concealed*
10	*arrested*				

6

Ask students to work with someone from the other group to answer the questions.
Check the answers round the class. Ask students with text A to answer about people from text B and vice versa.

Answers

Maria
1 She was offered a free holiday in Switzerland following an argument with her husband.
2 She smuggled cocaine.
3 She got fourteen years.

Janet
1 She was offered £2,000 and because she was in debt she said yes.
2 She smuggled a parcel of cocaine.
3 She got seven years.

Hazel
1 She didn't know she was carrying drugs and thought she was taking a parcel of Jamaican food to a friend's family.
2 She smuggled 13 kilos of cannabis.
3 She got six years.

Jefferson
1 He had debts of £10,000 so he did it because he was offered a large amount of money.
2 He smuggled heroin.
3 He got seven years.

7

Prepare students by eliciting the language used to give opinions:
I think, I feel that . . . , As far as I'm concerned, etc.
Write the phrases on the board so that students can refer to them.
Form groups of four or five. The students discuss the questions in their groups. Tell them that they have to give reasons for their opinions.
Several groups report their opinions back to the class.
Extend the activity by doing error correction and doing further practice of the language needed to give opinions.

Homework

Prepare by giving students prompts, eg:
Who? Why? What and where? How caught?

Practice *page 81*

Language Summary

At this level the passive will not be a new language area. Elicit how to form the passive and when to use it. Refer students to the Language Summary to refresh their memories.

1

Ask students to do Exercise 1 alone and then compare answers.

Answers

2 When you arrive at the airport your luggage is checked in and a seat is reserved for you by the ground attendant.
3 Your suitcases are taken to the plane and put into the hold of the aircraft by baggage handling staff.
4 Hand luggage is checked and passengers are searched by security staff.
5 During the flight passengers are looked after by flight attendants.

2

This gives more practice in using the active and passive. Ask students to do this exercise in pairs.

Answers

2	*was found*	3	*was marked*	4	*went*
5	*were waiting*	6	*watched*	7	*was taken*
8	*asked*	9	*was searched*	10	*was found*
11	*was cautioned*	12	*(was) taken*		

3

Brainstorm the stages of a journey by plane. Then students do the exercise, as a whole class activity, in pairs, or perhaps as a competition, to find which student or pair of students can place the most labels correctly in a given time, eg up to five minutes.

Answers

1	*information desk*	2	*check-in desk*
3	*flight attendants*	4	*baggage reclaim*
5	*shopping concourse*	6	*departure lounge*
7	*restaurant*	8	*security check*
9	*passport control*	10	*arrivals hall*
11	*meeting point*	12	*passengers*
13	*sniffer dogs*	14	*customs hall*

Lesson 2 *Life inside*

Aims: to find out about prison life and to discuss what makes a good prison and the rationale for sending people to prison.

Language focus

1 First conditional
If prisoners are sent to Chino, they **will have** the chance to become highly-paid commercial divers.
If you don't educate them, they**'ll** just **return** to crime.

2 Revision of *Wh-* questions
Who provides the facilities?
Where will prisoners work?

Skills focus

- **Reading** a newspaper article for specific information
- **Speaking:** a discussion about prison facilities

Vocabulary focus

- People in prisons: *prisoners, convicted criminals, inmates, convicts, patrols, armed guards*
- Prisons: *barbed wire fences, gun towers, sentences, mail bags, jail, release, rehabilitation*
- Diving: *deep-sea diving, commercial divers, five-metre deep tanks, decompression chamber, diving injuries, drown*

Review

A revision of the passive: play Twenty Questions.
A student chooses an item from everyday life, eg a machine, an article of clothing, food or drink. The other students must guess what it is by asking up to 20 Yes/No questions, using the present passive as much as possible. For example:
Is it something to wear? Is it worn outside?

Warmer

Put students into groups.
Either write the sentence below on the board in its jumbled form or put the words on individual cards and give each group a set.
Students have to reconstruct the original sentence.
breaking sent you to keep if for the long law time you'll prison be a
If you keep breaking the law, you'll be sent to prison for a long time.
This introduces the subject of the lesson and could also lead into the language focus explanation and exercises (see practice page 82).

1

Before allowing students to open their books, write the headline in jumbled form on the board. Or write each word from the headline on a separate card and give one card each to seven students. Ask them to come to the front of the class and with the help of the class arrange themselves into an order to make a logical headline.
Ask students to work in pairs to discuss what they think the article is about.
Elicit ideas quickly from several pairs before getting the students to open their books to read the first two paragraphs. Tell them not to worry about vocabulary they do not know, just skim the text to understand the gist.
Check whether any of the pairs had the right idea.

2

Before students read the complete article remind them again that they do not need to understand every word to understand the gist, which is all they need for the paragraph headings.
Allow students time to do this alone and then compare their answers with another student.

Answers

3 – 4	*Good money*
5 – 8	*Keeping prisoners out of jail*
9	*Who pays?*
10 – 11	*What the prisoners think*
12- 14	*High salaries, but a dangerous job*

3

Ask students to do this exercise in pairs. They may need to use dictionaries and/or refer to the vocabulary in Activity 4 to help them.

Answers

1 *Because it runs a successful rehabilitation scheme which teaches prisoners how to be deep-sea divers so that when they leave prison they are able to earn good money.*
2 *How to make mail-bags and car number plates and do car repairs.*
3 *They are able to earn more than $75,000 a year.*
4 *6% of Chino prisoners return to crime as compared to 75% of inmates in other Californian prisons.*
5 *The prison has some of its own equipment and some has been given by the United States Navy and by diving companies.*
6 *He loves teaching and diving but he thinks the job of diving is too dangerous.*

4

Ask students to work in pairs to do this exercise.
Start half the class at number 1 and the other half at 8, to work backwards.
After a short time ask pairs to work together to share their answers.

Answers

1	*inmates*	2	*rehabilitation scheme*	3	*convicts*
4	*achievement*	5	*self-esteem*	6	*former inmates*
7	*drown*	8	*suffocate*		

5

Refer to Lesson 1 in this unit where students gave their opinions. Elicit phrases to give opinions, to show agreement and disagreement. If necessary, write them on the board.
Before starting the activity look briefly at the first statement with the whole class to get some ideas.
Form groups of about four and give each member a letter, a, b, c, d. Choose one of these letters and tell those students that they will report from their group. (This ensures that the same students do not always report.)
You may have to help some groups with ideas.
Listen for the use of prepared phrases.
Each group reports back briefly. Write for and against ideas on the board.
This would be a suitable place to introduce the language focus point: first conditional. This will probably be revision. Refer students to Language Summary 1 on practice page 82. They should then do Exercises 1 and 2.

6

Ask students to remain in the same groups to decide on facilities necessary for a good prison.
Display the lists on the walls and ask students to move round to compare them.

Homework

To prepare students ask them about the layout of a letter of this type and put it on the board. It is a formal letter and should include:
greeting: *Dear Sir/Editor*
ending: *Yours faithfully*
useful phrases: *I read recently in your paper about . . . ; Are your readers aware that . . .* etc.

Practice *page 82*

Language Summary 1

Refer students to the text in Lesson 2 Activity 2, and ask them in pairs to see how quickly they can find all the examples of first conditionals. Refer them to the Language Summary to remind themselves of the structure.

1

Ask them to do Exercise 1 on their own.

Answers

2 *spends, won't have*
3 *will do, doesn't*
4 *will start, spends*
5 *does, will commit*
6 *will get arrested, will send, catch*
7 *will spend, continues*

2

Ask students to do this in pairs. Then ask them to make *If* sentences using ideas from the list in Lesson 2 Activity 6.

Possible answers

2 *If he isn't careful, he'll fall out of the boat/capsize.*
3 *If the explorer doesn't find an oasis/some water/get rescued soon, he'll die of thirst.*
4 *If she doesn't close her handbag, she'll lose her purse/someone will steal her purse.*
5 *If he doesn't stop talking and turn off the bath, he'll have a flood.*

Language Summary 2

In Unit 1 Lesson 2 *Wh-* questions were revised with the teacher wearing a label, on which were three answers. The students were asked to guess the questions.
Repeat this activity and write every question the students suggest on the board. Do not correct them.
Depending on the mistakes they make revise how to make *Wh-* questions by referring students to the Language Summary and looking back to Unit 1 Lesson 1.
Ask students to work in pairs to correct any mistakes on the board.
Give each student a label. Ask them to write three answers on their label. Ask students to work in pairs to find each other's questions.

3

Ask students to complete Exercise 3 alone and compare their answers with a partner.

Answers

3 *What do other jails teach inmates to do?*
4 *What have former inmates done?*
5 *Where do inmates learn to dive?*
6 *Who has given equipment to Chino Jail?*
7 *How long has the scheme been working for?*
8 *Why is Brian Emery in prison?*
9 *How many times has Tony Charles been in prison?*
10 *Why doesn't Paul Woodley want to be a diver?/Why wouldn't Paul Woodley want to be a diver?*

Lesson 3 *Punishment*

Aim: to discuss the appropriacy of sentences given to people who have committed crimes.

Language focus

Present perfect and past simple
He**'s been** unemployed for over 18 months.
A man **has stolen** some toys.
In the last three years Ms Madison **has left** her husband nine times.
He **stole** the toys just before Christmas.

Skills focus

- **Listening** to a discussion to make notes in order to complete a chart and do a dictation
- **Speaking:** a discussion to reach a majority decision about the sentences people should receive for crimes
- **Writing** a report on the punishment given for a crime, with reasons

Vocabulary focus

- Crimes: *armed robbery, arson, drink driving, manslaughter, rape, shoplifting, smuggling, theft*
- Punishments: *death penalty, life sentence, long/short prison sentence, probation, suspended prison sentence, fine*

Review

Display the letters from the Lesson 2 homework round the walls, or give them out in groups.
Ask students to look at the letters to check and correct layout, greetings, paragraphing, spelling, etc.

1

Use Activity 1 as a warmer. Ask students to work in pairs to make the list of crimes. The pair who have the longest list report back to the class. Write the crimes on the board. Add any others that other students have thought of.
Ask pairs to write the word for the person who commits each crime, eg burglary – burglar; arson – arsonist.
Extend the activity by giving students the word map from practice page 83 Exercise 3.

2

▭ Play the cassette through once for the students to listen for the answer to the gist questions.

Answers

1 *He has stolen some toys from a Department Store.*
2 *The man thinks he should go to prison for a short sentence or be fined and have a suspended sentence. The woman thinks he should pay for the toys and be put on probation.*

3

▭ Play the cassette through again. Ask students to make notes in the table and then compare their notes with another student.
Go through the answers with the class. If necessary play the cassette again.
N.B. *Reasons* refers to why he committed the crime.

Answers

Name	*Mark Thompson*
Occupation	*unemployed for 18 months*
Family	*he has children*
Crime	*stole toys from a shop*
Punishment	*He hasn't received a sentence yet, but it is the policy of the store to prosecute.*
Reasons	*He has been unemployed for 18 months and wanted his children to have some Christmas presents.*

4

Ask students to read the gapped text alone. They then try to fill in as many gaps as they can with a partner.
▭ Play the relevant part of the cassette and ask students to fill in the gaps alone.
Play it again and stop at any parts of the cassette that prove difficult.

Answers

Man:	*should go*
Woman:	*can't look, might do*
Man:	*should give*
Woman:	*should let, should be*

Ask for the students' opinions about a sentence for Mark Thompson. This leads into Activity 5 which asks students to decide on prison sentences for specific crimes.

5

Put the class into groups of four.
For this activity emphasise that they have to decide on the maximum sentence. Every case differs, but they cannot go above the maximum.
To make feedback efficient, give one group the crimes on separate cards and the punishments on different coloured card. Get this group to stick their cards onto the board. This gives a basis for feedback.
Ask for reasons for decisions, particularly if any vary greatly from the majority.

6

Refer back to the dictation in Activity 4. Elicit a phrase used when you want to give your opinion, eg: *I think . . .*
Extend the activity by asking for more phrases, eg: *I feel that; as far as I'm concerned* etc.
Again from the dictation elicit phrases expressing certainty/uncertainty; probability/possibility, eg: *perhaps, maybe, If he's in prison, he won't be able to look for a job.*
Extend the activity again by asking students for more phrases, eg: *I'm not sure if . . .*
You may also like to elicit phrases for contradicting other people's opinions and for giving reasons.

Or

Put a list of phrases on the board. Then give a list of headings:
Giving opinions
Expressing certainty/uncertainty/probability/possibility
Contradicting
Giving reasons
Ask students to work in pairs to decide which phrases go with each heading.
For the discussion, students form groups of four. Tell them that they have to agree as a group and be ready to give reasons for their decisions.
Give a time limit of ten to fifteen minutes. Monitor for the use of given phrases.
On the board write a chart for feedback with the name of each criminal and room for each group to write their punishment.
Ask groups for reasons for their decisions.

Homework

Prepare students by establishing why a report is written: to inform people about the case.
Elicit the information that should be included:
Name of accused
Details of crime
Information about the criminal
Punishment
Reasons for punishment
Agree on the length of the report.

Practice *page 83*

Language Summary

In Unit 2 Lesson 2 students met the present perfect to talk about a situation which began in the past and continues up to the present. Here the uses are extended.
Elicit facts about Mark Thompson's life to show how a situation in the present has a link with what has happened in the past.
Refer students to the Language Summary. Contrast the example about Ms Madison with the example about Mark Thompson which is in the past simple because we know when the event happened.

1

Ask students to do this exercise alone and then compare their answers with a partner.

Answers

made   stole   have been   haven't bought   was   have been have tried   didn't accept   offered

2

Ask students to work with a partner to do this.

Answers

2 *has been given*	3 *has admitted*	4 *broke out*
5 *spent*	6 *released*	7 *gave*
8 *claimed*	9 *said*	10 *did not know*
11 *gave*	12 *returned*	13 *has admitted*
14 *had*	15 *ended*	

3

Ask students to do the word map in pairs.
Extend the activity by getting students to mark the stress on the words. They may need to use a dictionary.

Answers

Weapons: *bomb, dagger, revolver*
Police: *constable, plain clothes detective, sergeant*
Criminals: *arsonist, burglar, hijacker, kidnapper, murderer, offender, rapist, thief*
Sentences: *life imprisonment, probation, suspended sentence*
Crimes: *arson, assault, burglary, fraud, hijacking, kidnapping, manslaughter, rape, robbery, shoplifting, theft, trespass*

The theme of this unit is the relationship between children who are high achievers, and their parents.

Lesson 1 *In business*

Aims: to find out about an unusual child and talk about the problems that may arise because of his individuality.

Language focus

1 *used to* + infinitive and *be/get used to* + *-ing* form
His father and I **used to run** a pub.
I**'m getting used to treating** him as an adult.
We**'re used to** all sorts.

2 *ago* and *for*
A year **ago** he opened Bow-Kays.
He's been an antique dealer **for** several years.

Skills focus

- **Reading** to make notes in order to complete a table
- **Listening** to someone talking about himself in order to complete a table

Vocabulary focus

- Age groups: *babyhood, childhood, teenage, middle age, old age*
- Stages in life: *education, work, get married, have children, retire*
- From the text: *antiques, spot, junk, interfere, swear*

Review

Write ten to fifteen words from the last unit on the board. Check that the students understand them.
Give students a minute to look at them and then cover them or rub them out. Ask students to work in pairs to spell the words correctly.

Warmer

Ask students to work in pairs to tell each other their earliest memory. Begin by telling them yours.

1

Ask students to do this alone, then move round to find another student who has the same age ranges.
Students' ideas may differ from yours and this could lead to discussion of how our ideas change with age.
Ask students to write the good and bad points and compare them with another pair. Several pairs report back to the class. Have a class discussion of how the students feel about getting older. This may be contrasted with your feelings.

2

Ask students to stay in the same pairs, and do the activity quickly. Get answers round the class, writing the ages on the board. Students give their reasons for their choices.

3

Ask students to work in pairs to discuss the picture. James is distinctive looking and students should be able to speculate easily. When students report back, raise their interest in preparation for the reading.

4

The first reading is a skim reading to confirm predictions, therefore students do not need to read in detail or to understand every word. You may like to give a time limit. Check if students' predictions were correct, if anything surprised them and if they would like to change the three adjectives they wrote to describe James.

5

Students will probably need to read the text again in order to do the vocabulary task. Ask students to work in pairs and discuss the meanings before using a dictionary.

Answers

1	*antiques*	2	*spot*	3	*junk*	4	*picked up*
5	*interfere*	6	*retired*	7	*swears*		

6

Ask students to work in pairs to complete as much of the table as they can. Go through the answers with the class and write the notes on the board.

Answers

Education   *went to school for 8 years; finished now; retired headmaster, Lionel Fanthorpe, teaches him 4 hours per week; says James too unusual for school*

Antiques   *antique dealer for several years; good at spotting valuable objects at jumble sales eg Royal Doulton statuette worth £4,000; bought junk jewellery for 10 pence, sold it for £8,000*

Flowers   *opened flower shop a year ago*

Relationships with family   *parents don't interfere, treat him like an adult*

7

▭ Play the cassette through once and ask students to complete the table alone. They then compare their notes with another student. Play the cassette again, stopping at any parts that they found difficult.

Answers

Education   *retired from school a year ago; only played football; he feels his mind was not used*
Clothes   *doesn't like jeans, scruffy clothes; has worn suits and ties since age 6*
Hobbies   *embroidery, talking to family*
Sports   *goes swimming for exercise*
Relationships   *doesn't like children, neither he nor his brother have friends of their own age*
Future   *saves money because wants to be rich, youngest ever Member of Parliament and then Prime Minister*

8

Form groups of four to talk about the three questions. Put two groups together to share their ideas.
Note: It might interest the students to receive an update about James.

James went to America to appear in a chat show, the Oprah Winfrey show. When he arrived home his father had been imprisoned for five years for fraud and arson because he tried to burn down one of his businesses in order to claim the insurance and pay enormous debts. James is now embroidering a pillowcase with 'I love you dad' on it, to give his father in prison. The florist shop has failed due to the recession and the local education authority are investigating why James has stopped having lessons from Lionel Fanthorpe. The family are now very isolated and their house is often vandalised by local boys. In a newspaper article about James they ask the question: 'Was James Harries born or was he made?'

Homework

Elicit from several students who they would like to write about. Look at the structure of the text in Activity 4. Remind students that when we introduce a new subject into a piece of writing we usually start a new paragraph.

Practice *page 84*

Language Summary 1

Read aloud the explanation about *used to*.
Ask students to look back at the texts in the lesson and to find all the examples of *used to*. Ask individual students to read the sentences aloud, then drill all the students together.
Explain that in the pronunciation of *used to*, the d is silent when we speak. Also point out that there is no final d in the negative and interrogative form of *use*, eg:
He didn't use to play with other boys.
Elicit things students used to do but don't do now, eg:
I used to suck my thumb.
Do the same for *be/get used to*.
Elicit examples using *-ing* and a noun, eg:
I'm used to doing my homework every evening.
We're used to using computers nowadays.

1

Ask students to do Exercise 1 alone. Check the answers with the whole class.

Answers

| 2 *run* | 3 *being* | 4 *suffer* | 5 *being* |
| 6 *think* | 7 *teaching* | 8 *dealing* | |

2

Ask students to work with a partner to do this exercise.

Answers

2 *used to buy*	3 *used to go*
4 *am used to studying*	5 *used to do*
6 *am used to helping*	7 *are used to working*
8 *used to have*	

3

This will be a revision for students. Ask them to look at Language Summary 2 and do the exercise alone.

Answers

3 *James opened Bow-Kays one year ago.*
4 *James has been in business for one year.*
5 *James has not gone to school for over a year.*
6 *James left school over a year ago.*
7 *James stayed at school for almost eight years.*
8 *Lionel started teaching James a year ago.*

Extend the activity by asking students to work in groups to write four general knowledge questions to ask each other about their country. Give examples to guide students on form, eg: *How long has this government been in power?*
How long has X been president?

4

Ask students to do this in pairs. They may need a dictionary.

Answers

flower arranging, vase
collecting, antiques
football, cup final
dancing, partner
cooking, recipe
gardening, plants
art, paints
bird-watching, binoculars
opera, aria

Lesson 2 *In control*

Aim: for students to give opinions about how much control parents should have over their children's lives.

Language focus

Comparatives and superlatives
This is a much **healthier** way of eating.
The **greatest** athletes are not just born, but can be made.

Skills focus

● **Speaking:** fluency – exchanging opinions about parental control
● **Reading** a newspaper article for specific information
● **Listening** to a monologue for the main ideas and to infer meaning

Vocabulary focus

● Food: *pureed parsley, carrots, broccoli, spinach, unpasteurised skimmed milk, tuna, low-fat cheese, milk shakes, fizzy drinks, sweets, candies, fruit toast snack*
● Contents of food: *protein, vitamin supplement, nutrients*
● Problems: *stresses, strains, damaging, psychological pressure*

Review

Build on the homework from Lesson 1. Put students into pairs. Ask one student to close their eyes and try to describe their partner's appearance from memory. Their partner can help by asking questions and commenting.
Students then read each other's description of a family member from the homework of the previous lesson.

Warmer

Before students open their books ask them if they think they would like to have children. Why/why not? How many? What are the difficulties, if any, of bringing up children?

1

Note: Before starting this lesson, ask students to cover the text about Mikhail.
Ask students to think about the statements individually and then discuss their answers with a partner. They will probably draw from their own experiences with their parents.
Ask pairs to tell the class if they think parents should be strict or not. They will probably want to qualify their decision according to what they think strict means.
Keep a score on the board to see what the majority feeling is. This would be a suitable place to introduce the language point. Refer students to the Language Summary on practice page 85.

They can also do Exercise 1.

2

It is important that students haven't looked at the article or the prediction task will not be valid.
Ask students to predict in pairs. Get suggestions quickly from several pairs.

3

Ask students to skim the text alone to confirm their predictions. They are reading for gist so they do not need to understand every word.

4

Ask students to read the article again alone, but to discuss the answers with a partner and to help each other with vocabulary. Tell them to underline five words they do not understand and ask their partner for help. They should only use a dictionary if their partner cannot help.
For feedback ask one pair to give the answer to 1 and then ask them to choose another pair to answer 2, and so on.

Answers

1 *protein: eggs, low-fat cheese, tuna, chicken, yoghurt*
vegetables: pureed parsley, carrots, broccoli, spinach
He doesn't eat much red meat.
2 *sweets/candies, fizzy drinks, hamburgers, milkshakes*
3 *Because his father believes it is the healthiest diet for a growing body.*
4 *Mikhail calls his exercise programme games. They are to make him into a great athlete. His father believes you can make great athletes. Mikhail plays the games for three hours after breakfast.*
5 *His father.*
6 *His father says he is.*
7 *He is Mikhail's elder brother. He is 1 metre 95 cms tall and is very muscular. He is an American football star.*

This would be a suitable point for the students to do Exercise 2 on practice page 85.

5

Put the students into groups of four.
Lead into this activity by telling of your experience of being made to do something by your parents, eg practising a musical instrument. Encourage students to think about themselves: Could they have done better if . . . ?
Tell groups to elect a spokesperson before they begin. That person will report for their group.
Write students' ideas on the board.

6

▣ Play the cassette through once. Get answers to the questions from round the class.

Answers

He doesn't think the programme is a good idea.

If children do too much sport they can develop unnatural stresses and strains which can damage their bodies. Their muscles may be permanently damaged. Also no account is taken of Mikhail's opinions and this can cause psychological pressures.

7

Refer to the board to see if the problems students thought of in Activity 5 match those mentioned by the child care expert. 📼 Play the cassette through again and ask students to work with a partner to answer the questions.

Answers

1 *True – statistics in the USA show that a lot of American children are more unhealthy now than in the past.*
2 *False – it's the muscles you can damage.*
3 *False – if you continually overuse muscles you can do permanent damage to them.*
4 *False – experts believe that when parents have such control over their children and do not allow them to have any opinions of their own it puts them under great psychological pressure.*
5 *True – he is a millionaire and is only 21 years old.*
6 *False – he has had to live very differently from other children.*
7 *False – he has only had training in American football and can do nothing else.*

8

When students have compared their statements with those of another pair, display the lists on the walls and let everyone walk round to see all of them.
This would be an appropriate place to introduce the language point, if you have not already done so. Students may need to use the comparative and superlative for homework.

Homework

Prepare students by referring back to the statements in Activity 1. Elicit questions, or if there is time, divide the class. Ask half to write the questions to ask a child; the other half to make questions to ask the parent.
Pairs from each half form groups of four to share their questions.

Practice *page 85*

Language Summary

This will probably be revision for the students. However they often make mistakes when using comparatives and superlatives, so insist on accuracy.
Refer students to the Language Summary.

1

After a few minutes go round the class quickly asking each student to give you a sentence using the words from the box in Exercise 1, eg: *I am taller than Ariana.*
The next student has to use *tall* with a superlative, eg: *Ivan is the tallest in the class.*

Answers

adjective	comparative	superlative
hard	harder	hardest
tall	taller	tallest
strict	stricter	strictest
big	bigger	biggest
fat	fatter	fattest
fit	fitter	fittest
thin	thinner	thinnest
late	later	latest
sporty	sportier	sportiest
happy	happier	happiest
heavy	heavier	heaviest
healthy	healthier	healthiest
unhealthy	unhealthier	unhealthiest
angry	angrier	angriest
relaxing	more relaxing	most relaxing
difficult	more difficult	most difficult
good	better	best
bad	worse	worst

2

Ask students to do this alone and then compare answers with a partner.

Answers

3 *the healthiest* 4 *healthier* 5 *sportier*
6 *heavier, fatter, fitter* 7 *the greatest* 8 *the worst*
9 *the most difficult* 10 *harder* 11 *more relaxing*
12 *the most relaxing* 13 *The latest* 14 *more difficult*
15 *the hardest* 16 *angriest*

3

Ask students to work in pairs to do this. Extend the activity by getting them to think of as many other examples as they can. You could make it into a class competition.

Answers

a bottle of wine   *a tin of tuna*   *a carton of yoghurt*
a packet of biscuits   *a jar of honey*   *a box of chocolates*

Lesson 3 *Courting tragedy*

Aims: to understand problems young people have when trying to achieve international success in sport and to give advice to such people and their parents in the form of a letter.

Language focus

1 Linking words: conjunctions; contrast, reason and result linkers
   We have **also** started to have rows.
   It has been hard **because** we don't have much money.
   Although I love spending time training, I don't have many friends.
   I feel she hates me **whereas** I do my best to show her I love her.

2 *should* and *ought to* for advice
   You **should** try to understand her problems.

Skills focus

- **Listening** for specific points and in order to complete a table, and for pieces of advice
- **Writing** a letter of advice
- **Speaking:** giving opinions

Vocabulary focus

- Injuries: *break, bruise, fracture, sprain, cut*
- Parts of the body: *cartilage, elbow, knee, leg, muscle, ligament*
- Psychological problems: *anxiety, depression, stress, tension*

Warmer

Writer the parts of the body on labels. Include *calf, hip, pelvis, instep, coccyx*. Divide the class into groups and give each group a set of labels. Ask each group to choose a 'demonstrator'. The labels will be stuck onto this person. Set a four-minute time limit for labels to be stuck in the correct places.

1

Ask students to work in pairs to put the vocabulary under the correct headings. Encourage them to help each other with meanings. Ask them to mark the stress on the words.
Give one pair the words on card so that they can group them on the board. This makes feedback easy. Drill the words.
To give some practice using the words, ask students to talk in pairs about anyone they know who has had any of the injuries/problems mentioned.

Answers

injuries: *break, bruise, cut, fracture, sprain, muscle*
parts of the body: *cartilage, elbow, knee, leg ligament*
psychological problems: *anxiety, depression, stress, tension*

2

Ask students to talk in pairs to discuss these questions.

Answers

She is a tennis champion and she is holding the cup because she has won the women's singles tennis championships at Wimbledon.

3

Get one person in each pair to write down the answers. Get answers from around the class. You could write all the ideas on the board for students to refer to during the listening.
Play the cassette through once for students to compare their ideas with those on the cassette.

4

Ask students to work in pairs to try to fill in as much as they can of the table before you play the cassette again.
Play the cassette for students to check what they have written.
Ask four pairs to write their answers about one of the tennis players on the board and use these for feedback.

Answers

Tracy Austin
successes	*won US open Championship at 16 Number 2 player in world*
physical problems	*stress fracture in back; gave up tennis before she was 21*
life now	*tennis commentator for American TV; is happy*

Jennifer Capriati
family	*argued with parents at 15*
school	*didn't have time to do any schoolwork*

Monika Seles
early life	*moved from Yugoslavia to USA when 13*
family relationships	*relies completely on father, brother and mother*

Hana Mandlikova
relationships	*lonely so married when 24 and divorced 2 years later*

You may wish to look at the Language Summary 2 on practice page 86 and ask students to do Exercise 2 here as they need to use the language of advice in the discussion in Activity 5.

5

Play the cassette through once. Students should note the advice the coach gives. You may want to go through the advice before going on to the next stage. When students report their answers insist that they use the modals *should* and *ought to*. They then decide whether or not they agree with each piece of advice. Next ask students to discuss their views with a partner. If you prefer, divide the class into groups of four for the discussion. Put groups together to compare their views and get feedback from each group. Comment on any mistakes when using modals.

Answers

Refer to Tapescript.

6

Before you look at the letters with the students refer to Language Summary 1 on practice page 86. Point out that sometimes we want to use a stronger word than *but* to make a contrast. Ask students to do Exercise 1 on practice page 86. Divide the class into A and B. Give each group the corresponding letter from the lesson. Ask students if they can find examples in their letter of ideas linked with *although, however*, etc.

Make sure that each group answers the questions in Activity 6.

Answers

Letter A: *From a child, a daughter. She has had an argument with her father because she spends all her time training and no time with friends.*

Letter B: *From a father. He wants his child to do well at swimming and she has started to rebel.*

7

Prepare students by asking them if they read the problem pages in magazines. Find out if anyone has ever written to one. Elicit greetings and suitable opening and finishing sentences for these kinds of letters.

Tell students that their letter will be read by others so the writing and layout must be clear.

Monitor and help with grammar and other problems as necessary. Set a time limit so that everyone finishes at the same time.

Join A and B pairs to exchange letters and replies. Ask students to discuss each other's advice. According to how the discussion is going, you may like to form groups of eight to expand the discussion.

All the groups report back to share all the opinions. Correct errors in the language and pronunciation used.

Extend the activity by asking pairs to correct each other's letters. Display them in a problem page book.

Homework

Prepare students and refresh memories, by asking them to talk to the person next to them for one minute about James Harries in Lesson 1 of this unit.

Then ask them to turn to the student on the other side of them to talk for one minute about Mikhail from Lesson 2.

Practice *page 86*

1

Ask students to find examples of the linkers in the letter that they did not read in Lesson 3 Activity 6.

Ask students to work alone to do the exercise and take it in turns to read the answers to each other. The listener checks the answers.

Answers

1 *However, because, and, also*
2 *because, Although, and, but*
3 *whereas, However, Although*
4 *Although, and, however*

2

Point out the slightly more emphatic use of ought to when giving advice. Ask students to work in pairs to finish the sentences. They then compare their answers with another pair.

3

Ask students to work in pairs to complete the table. Ask three pairs to write answers to one column each on the board.

Answers

agreement	uncertainty	disagreement
Absolutely!	*I'm not sure.*	*I can't accept that.*
I agree.	*Perhaps you're right.*	*Impossible!*
Of course!	*Probably.*	*No, I don't think so.*
There's no doubt.*	*Well, it depends.*	*Of course not!*
Yes, definitely!		*There's no doubt.**
Yes, I agree.		
Yes, I think so too.		

*There's no doubt is a strong reinforcer that can be used to agree or disagree.

Prepare students for the second part of the exercise by practising some of the phrases together.

Ask students to do the stress exercise in pairs. Emphasise that they cannot do this silently.

Write the words on the board with the correct stress marked and drill the phrases.

Answers

one stress	two stresses	three stresses
Of course!	*Perhaps you're right.*	*No, I don't think so.*
I agree.	*I can't accept that.*	*Yes, I think so too.*
Impossible!	*I'm not sure.*	
Probably.	*Of course not!*	
Absolutely!	*There's no doubt.*	
	Well, it depends.	
	Yes, definitely!	
	Yes, I agree.	

Give further practice by asking students to form a circle. You stand in the middle and make a statement to students in turn. For example: *The moon is made of cheese.*

Students have to reply using one of the statements from Exercise 3.

The theme of this unit is the growing trend towards alternative lifestyles in all areas of our lives.

Lesson 1 *Alternative healing*

Aims: to look at alternative methods for curing bad habits.

Language focus

Reporting verbs
The acupuncturist **told me** that I would feel calmer.
She **admitted** that a lot of people felt that.
She **advised me** not to go home immediately.

Skills focus

- **Reading** a diary and reading instructions in order to perform a task
- **Speaking:** comparing and exchanging information
- **Listening** for specific information
- **Writing** a questionnaire about habits

Vocabulary focus

- Healing: *acupuncture, acupressure, Shiatsu, massage, acupuncturist, needles, manipulate, pressure, pulse, energy, Chi, a practice, a practitioner*
- Problems: *insomnia, backache, nail biting, overwork, to be stressed out*

Warmer

Write the word *alternative* on the board. Divide the class into pairs and give them two minutes to make as many words as they can from the word on the board, eg *native, alter, late* etc.

1

Do not let students open their books! Read, or write on the board the information from the speech bubble and ask students to guess what the subject is. Find out if anyone has had acupuncture or knows anyone who has. Ask them to work in small groups to write anything they know about it. 🔲 If they do not know anything about it tell them to listen to the cassette to find out as much as they can.

2

🔲 Play the cassette through again. Ask students to answer individually. They then compare their answers with a partner.

Answers

1 *False – it unblocks the flow of energy.* 2 *False.*
3 *True (insomnia).*   4 *False – one to twenty are used.*
5 *False – everybody has the same sort.*

3

Make sure students look at the picture and make suggestions before they read the first extract.

4

This is a short jigsaw reading activity.
Put the class into three groups, A, B and C.
Tell the students to read their appropriate text and work together to answer as many questions as they can. Move round the groups to check the answers.
Re-form the groups so that there is an A, B and C in each group. Tell them to share their information with the other members of the group.
Report back orally round the class. Insist that students use reporting verbs to give the information.

Answers

Text A

1 *She asked Helen how many cups of coffee she drank.*
2 *Five, in her wrists and ankles.*
3 *She felt relaxed. Her arms felt longer and her legs shorter.*
4 *She felt relaxed for the rest of the day.*
5 *No.*

Text B

1 *She asked her about her job.*
2 *Some round her feet and two between her middle and ring fingers on her right hand.*
3 *Not calm.*
4 *Uncomfortable.*
5 *No.*

Text C

1 *She asked if Helen had noticed any changes since her last session.*
2 *Three in her right foot and one in her right arm.*
3 *Tense to begin with and then sleepy.*
4 *She still felt sleepy after two days.*
5 *No.*

5

Tell students to stay in their same groups of three to answer these questions.
Report back orally round the class and insist they use reporting verbs to give the information.

Answers

1 *She was surprised by the questions that she was asked and the immediate feeling of sleepiness she felt when the practitioner moved one needle in the third session.*
2 *No, although she did stop biting her nails for a short period.*
3 *No correct answer, students' opinion.*

To prepare for the next activity, brainstorm other so-called bad habits.
You may like to introduce the Language Summary on practice page 87 here before moving on to the questionnaire.

6

Ask students to work in pairs to write the questionnaire, but tell everyone to write down the questions.

Students do the interviews individually. Make sure that they all get a chance to interview and be interviewed.

Collate results on the board under headings:

Habit, Have tried to stop – Yes/No, Methods, Success/Failure

7

Ask students to raise their hands as soon as they have answered the questions. Then stop everyone and get the answers from the student who finished first.

Answers

1 *Quite strong.*
2 *About five minutes on each side.*
3 *Take deep breaths. As you breathe in relax the pressure, and apply it as you breathe out.*

8

Ask students to try the acupressure on each other.

You may like to introduce the language focus here, before preparing for the homework.

Challenge students to recall things from the lesson, for example, about Helen, the acupuncturist, the teacher, other students. See if they can remember about twelve things, eg:

The acupuncturist advised Helen to rest before she went.

You asked us if we knew the answer to the puzzle in Activity 1.

Write their examples on the board exactly as they say them. Look particularly for the use of reporting verbs. If they haven't used any you will need to do some remedial teaching on reported speech.

If they have used some refer students to the Language Summary on practice page 87 and see if they can change the verbs on the board so that they are more varied/correct.

Homework

Decide with students how detailed the diary is to be (note form, sentences?). They can look at Helen's diary extracts in Activities 3–5.

Prepare students by getting them to divide up areas in their notebooks into 7 days and mark the date at the top of each section.

Practice *page 87*

Language Summary

Refer students back to Helen's diary extracts in Lesson 1, Activities 3–5, and ask them to underline or note all the examples of different reporting verbs. They should look for different patterns of use and try to group them.

Go through the Language Summary to confirm the different patterns.

1

Ask students to do this exercise in pairs and check the answers around the class.

Answers

2 *Helen complained that she often got headaches.*
3 *Helen told the acupuncturist that she'd worked in an office for about three years.*
4 *Helen explained that she had never really liked the job.*
5 *Helen begged the acupuncturist not to hurt her.*
6 *Helen promised that she would try to stop biting her nails.*
7 *Helen admitted that (she was sorry) but she hadn't stopped biting her nails.*
8 *Helen said that she would continue the treatment for another month.*
9 *Helen explained that she would have to check her diary before making another appointment.*
10 *The acupuncturist advised her to eat fewer carbohydrates and more fresh vegetables.*
11 *The acupuncturist warned Helen not to drink more than two cups of coffee a day/that she should not drink more than two cups of coffee a day.*

2

Ask students to do this in pairs. They take it in turns to read the reported sentence while their partner tries to say the direct speech immediately. Then ask students to write them down.

Answers

2 *You should try to stay calm.*
3 *My advice is that you should drink less coffee/I advise you to drink less coffee.*
4 *We promise not to laugh.*
5 *Thank you for not hurting me/Thank you, it didn't hurt.*
6 *You will sleep better (now).*
7 *You will have to give up smoking.*
8 *Please could you try and stop before the next session.*

3

Answers

*acupressure   acupuncture   acupuncturist   aerobics
alternative   centimetres   extraordinary   insomnia
practice   practitioner*

4

Make this into a competition with students working in pairs. Tell them that the words are to be found horizontally and vertically.

Answers

Across: CALF, WAIST, KNEE, LEG, PALM, TOE, WRIST, FINGER
Down: NECK, FOOT, SHOULDER, NAIL, THIGH
Diagonal: ANKLE

Lesson 2 *Alternative eating*

Aim: to discuss the arguments for and against vegetarianism.

Language focus

Past simple and past perfect
> I **became** a vegetarian six years ago. Before that I **had** always **eaten** meat.
> I **decided** one day that I **had eaten** enough meat in my life.

Skills focus

- **Listening** for information in order to complete a table
- **Speaking:** expressing opinions and doing a roleplay to persuade people to your way of thinking
- **Writing:** taking notes on someone talking about being a vegetarian

Vocabulary focus

- Diet: *vegetarian, vegetarianism, meat-eater, health foods, well-balanced*
- Nutrition: *vitamins, minerals, proteins, nutrients, natural sources*
- Foods: *rice, coffee, cream, frozen/fresh vegetables, liver, milk, crisps, nuts, potatoes, sausages, steak, tea, white rice, yoghurt, biscuits*

Review

Groups of four compare diaries. Ask students to focus on habits mentioned: bedtimes and amounts of sleep. Feedback round the group.

Warmer

Write a tongue-twister on the board, then more quickly, eg: *Mixed biscuits, mixed biscuits*. Elicit the topic of the lesson: food.

1

Ask students to work in pairs to discuss the cartoon. Get opinions about it from the whole class. Ask pairs to agree on the foods they consider to be healthy. To help with feedback ask one pair to write their choices on the board.

Answers

> There may be some discussion, but these foods are generally considered to be unhealthy: *cake, coffee, cream, crisps, lemonade, sausages*
> Others are considered healthy: *beans, bread, brown rice, fish, fresh vegetables, liver, nuts, potatoes*
> *The remainder should not be eaten in too large quantities.*

2

Ask students to stay in their pairs to write down the food they ate yesterday. Tell them to try to remember everything.

Do not draw attention to anyone who may be embarrassed, but find a healthy and an unhealthy eater.

3

Ask students to work in groups and ask each group to elect a secretary to write the reasons down.

4

Play the cassette through once. Ask students to work in their groups to compare their reasons with those on the cassette. Groups report back to the class with any reasons they mentioned but Kate didn't.

5

Play the cassette through again. Ask students to work alone to complete the table, then compare notes in groups.

Answers

> **Why Kate gave up eating meat:** *She went to Argentina on holiday and ate meat all the time. When she arrived home she was given roast beef and she realised that she did not want to eat meat again.*

> **Why other people give up eating meat:** *religion, dislike of animal farming methods*

> **How Kate feels now:** *much healthier, better skin, doesn't get colds and sore throats as much*

> **Other people's attitudes to vegetarians:** *Some people think it's strange, and are angry about it. Some people think the diet would be boring.*

6

Ask students to work with a partner. Several pairs report back to the class.

7 and 8

There is some quite difficult vocabulary here. Encourage students to try to find the reasons for not being a vegetarian without using a dictionary.
Ask some students to report what they have found. Then ask them to work in pairs to do Activity 8 by guessing from context. Then, they may want to look again at their reasons.

Answers 7

> *The body needs many nutrients and the advertisement implies you can't get them all without meat, which is full of them.*
> *Meat is a natural source of vitamins and minerals.*

Answers 8

> **1** *b*   **2** *c*   **3** *f*   **4** *d*   **5** *e*   **6** *a*

9

It is important that students think about this carefully and get plenty of reasons on both sides, because they will need the

ideas for the roleplay. You may like to divide the class into vegetarians and meat eaters to do this activity.
Write all the ideas on the board so that everyone has access to them during the roleplay.

10

Prepare for this by getting the vegetarians to work together to share ideas and likewise the meat-eaters. You may like students to choose which they would like to be, although you may have to make adjustments if more choose one side.
This would be a useful place to look at the Language Summary on practice page 88, and also for students to do Exercise 3. This looks at useful language for a 'for and against' discussion like the one in Activity 8.
Tell students that at the end you will find out who has changed their mind. During the activity collect errors.
Comment on the good points of the roleplay and then on any errors. Include ways in which students could extend their vocabulary and widen the type of language they use.

Homework

Prepare students by eliciting what they consider to be the best of their country's food. Ask students to write the menu out properly and decorate it if they want to.

Practice *page 88*

Language Summary

Draw the time line on the board and talk the students through the explanation. Elicit examples from their lives.

1

Ask students to do the exercise alone and compare their answers in pairs.

Answers

2 *arrived*	**3** *had forgotten*	**4** *arrived*
5 *had started*	**6** *had gone*	**7** *found, had forgotten*

Extend the activity by playing past participle bingo:
Ask students to draw a bingo card of 3 x 3 squares with each square large enough to contain a word.
Write on the board a list of about fifteen verbs – as many from the lesson as you can, but make them irregular.
Ask students to choose nine of these at random and write each verb in one of the squares.
Either you or a student calls out the past participle of these verbs at random and students cross out the corresponding verb. The first student to complete a line vertically, horizontally or diagonally calls out Bingo! and wins.

2

Ask students to work with a partner to do the exercise.
To extend the activity, read the text to the students, asking them to mark the words that you stress.
In pairs ask them to take it in turns to read the text while the listener follows to see if the stress is in the correct place.

Answers

3 *went*	**4** *arrived*	**5** *had already prepared*
6 *had drunk*	**7** *sat*	**8** *had looked*
9 *went*	**10** *knew*	**11** *had prepared*
12 *did not know*	**13** *did not want*	**14** *had had*
15 *said*	**16** *rushed*	

3

Ask students to work in pairs to complete the exercise. Discuss with students when you would use the phrases they crossed out. Ask them to work in pairs to write a dialogue including at least three of these phrases and to perform it.

Answers

B: *I disagree.*
A: *But you can't say that.*
B: *That's not true.*
A: *I don't think you understand my point.*
B: *That may be true.*

4

You may like to keep this for the Review in the next lesson.
Ask students to work in pairs to put the words under the correct headings and to add two words of their own to each group.
Ask students to mark the stress on the words. They may need to use a dictionary. Practise the pronunciation with them.

Answers

vegetables	dairy products	meat and fish	other
*au*bergine	*cheese*	*chops*	*cof*fee
beans	*cream*	*cod*	*eggs*
*cauli*flower	*skim*med milk	*lamb*	*flour*
*cour*gettes	*yog*hurt	*liver*	*herb*
*cu*cumber		*saus*ages	*nuts*
leeks		*tripe*	*rais*ins
*spin*ach		*veal*	*rice*
*toma*toes			*spa*ghetti
			*sultan*as
			tea

Lesson 3 *Alternative thinking*

Aims: to find out about different ways to cope when things go wrong, and to lay out a letter correctly.

Language focus

1 Adjective prefixes
Matthew felt very **un**happy.
Being **im**patient only causes stress.

2 Articles
The family always kept **the** cup in the cupboard.

Skills focus

- **Listening** to a visualisation and ordering information
- **Writing** a letter requesting information

Vocabulary focus

- Adjectives: *afraid, astonished, astounded, excited, frightened, happy, puzzled, surprised, terrified, impatient, unhappy, insensitive, intolerant*
- Alternatives: *telepathy, psychic, medium, healer, astrology, poltergeist, psychic investigator, fate, healing workshops, self-healing, positive energy, a mystical experience, automatic writing*

Review

Display the menus from the homework from Lesson 2 round the room. Students walk round to choose the menu which has the best balance and includes good examples of the country's dishes.

Or

Ask students to work in groups of three. Ask one of them to be the waiter and use his/her menu as though in a restaurant. The other two are the customers.

1

It is appropriate to use Activity 1 as the warmer as it introduces the idea of a different, more relaxed way of approaching life.
If your students have never experienced a visualisation before they may be a bit giggly. Try not to tell them off because it will spoil the atmosphere. Just speak calmly and get everyone to relax. Maybe ask them to do some deep breathing first, and settle them down – they may like to put their heads on their desks.
▭ Play the cassette through once.

2

When the cassette has finished quietly ask the class to talk in pairs and tell each other about what they saw and how they felt. Some students may say that they felt silly. Don't dismiss this but say that it is probably because it was the first time.
Get feedback from several students, although be careful because some may not want the whole class to share their experience.

3

You could list the words under two headings, *positive* and *negative*.
When you have the list on the board ask the students when/why one would use visualisation.

4

Before doing the listening exercise, make sure that students understand the meaning of all the adjectives.
Ask students to take it in turns to mime one of the words so that the class can identify the word that he or she has chosen.
▭ Play the cassette through once and ask the students to work alone to tick the adjectives in the text. Ask students to compare their answers in pairs.

Answers

Adjectives used in the text are: *astounded, terrified, frightened, puzzled, excited*

5

Ask students to work in pairs to try to put the events in order before listening to the cassette again. Students may need help with some of the vocabulary in the ten statements.
▭ Play the cassette through once and ask students to work with their partner to finish putting the events in order.
Check the answers by asking students to take it in turns to read the statements in their correct order.

Answers

The order is: 2, 4, 1, 3, 7, 6, 10, 9, 8, 5

6

Ask students to work in pairs to write their questions.
Ask several pairs for examples.
Next, ask students to scan the article to see if there are answers to their questions.
Get feedback from students to see what they found.

7

There is a lot of information in this article so give students plenty of time to read it carefully.

Ask students to work together to help each other with vocabulary and then to complete the summary. It will help students to do the exercise if you tell them that they will often need to use phrases from the text and not just single words to fill the gaps.

Answers

1 *cancer*   2 *healthy*   3 *the weak cells*   4 *get better*
5 *die*   6 *other healers* 7 *the boys and girls upstairs*

8

Prepare students by telling them what surprised you. Give them time to think about their answers alone before mingling with the class to find someone who feels the same.
Get feedback from several pairs.

9

Ask students to work with a partner to put the letter into the correct order.
Write the correct letter on the board.

Answers

Dear Mr Manning,
I saw an article in this week's copy of Best about you and your centre.
I am very interested in your method of helping and healing people who are suffering.
I would be grateful if you would send me more information about your services, including cost and how to make an appointment.
I look forward to hearing from you soon.
Yours sincerely,
Erica Aguila

Homework

Elicit subjects students may be interested in. For example, a sport, a fan club, holidays.
Tell students that the letter should be correctly laid out and properly structured. They should refer to the letter in Activity 9.

Practice *page 89*

1

Elicit the opposite of happy. You may need to refer students to the text in Activity 6 of Lesson 3, as they may suggest sad.
See whether any of the class know the name for the *un-* part of unhappy (a prefix).
Dictate the words from the box in Exercise 1. Ask students to work in groups to find the opposites.
Check the answers and get the students to group the words according to the prefixes.

Answers

opposites formed with un-	opposites formed with im-	opposites formed with in-
unconscious	impossible	insensitive
unhappy	impatient	
unhealthy		
unkind		
unlucky		
unusual		
unnecessary		

2

This exercise gives practice in using the vocabulary from Exercise 1. Ask students to work with a partner. Check the answers with the whole class.

Answers

2 *unhappy*   3 *impatient*   4 *unusual*   5 *unconscious*
6 *unhealthy* 7 *unnecessary* 8 *unlucky*   9 *impossible*

3

Refer students to Language Summary 2. Ask them to work on Exercise 3 alone.
Check the answers round the class. If there are a lot of mistakes you may need to do some remedial teaching.

Answers

2 *The*   3 *(–)*   4 *(–)*   5 *(–)*   6 *(–)*
7 *A*   8 *The*   9 *an*   10 *a*

4

Ask students to work in pairs to do the exercise and also to mark the stress on the words. They may need to use a dictionary.
Drill the words if necessary.

Answers

2 *a medium* 3 *a healer*   4 *telepathy* 5 *astrology* 6 *a psychic*

The theme of this unit is looking at relationships between the sexes and thinking about what it would be like to be somebody different.

Lesson 1 *Could they be the same person?*

Aims: to compare relationships between twins and to compare family relationships in general.

Language focus

1 *both, either, neither/nor*
We **both** won prizes.
Neither Pauline **nor** Diana liked being a twin.
Ask **either** of them a question, the answer will be the same.

2 *so did . . ., neither/nor did . . .*
I absolutely hated it and **so did** Diana.
Keith didn't like that and **neither did** Clive.

Skills focus

- **Reading** an article for the main idea and for detail
- **Listening** to a twin talking about her life, for specific information
- **Speaking:** comparing family relationships

Vocabulary focus

- Twins: *identical, the same seed, non-existent differences, practically nil, jealous, same mannerisms, Siamese twins, simultaneously*
- Medical: *bronchitis, to be laid up with something, stitches, tonsils, operation, ribs, pain, prescription*
- The services: *army, conscripted, merchant navy*

Review

This is a vocabulary review and a way of extending students' knowledge.
Give students two prefixes, one from the previous lesson and one new one such as *re-* or *dis-*. Ask students to work in pairs to write down all the words they know which begin with these prefixes. Pairs share their lists with another pair.

Warmer

This puzzle introduces the theme of the unit, twins, and also practises asking questions. Write the puzzle on the board:
A woman committed a crime. The police arrested her and took her to court. The judge didn't know what to do about her.
Tell the class to read it and ask you questions about it. You answer Yes, No, or Not important.
Ask students to correct each other's questions and do not answer unless the question is correct. Refuse to answer Wh- questions.

When a student finds the answer make sure everyone understands it.

Answer

The woman was a Siamese twin whose attached twin would have automatically been involved, even though innocent. (Students may want to discuss whether the judge would have to acquit a clearly guilty person.)

1

You may have twins in the class. You will have to decide how much you want to focus on them.
Tell students to work in pairs to discuss the questions. Pairs report back to the class to find the general consensus about whether twins feel each other's pain, etc, and to find any interesting stories about twins.

2

▭ Play the cassette through once and ask students to work alone to answer the gist questions.
Go through the answers with the whole class.

Answers

1 *Yes.*
2 *No.*
3 *Yes, and often their mother also had the same material.*
4 *No.*

3

▭ Play the cassette through again and ask students to work with a partner to answer the questions.
During feedback get as much detail as possible about the twins following the True/False answer.

Answers

1 *True – Diana was born first and the second baby was a shock because nobody realised that their mother was expecting twins.*
2 *False – she was very small and cried all the time.*
3 *False – even though they did not like acting they were made to be in the school play because they looked so similar.*
4 *False – they won one each but received the same book as their prize.*
5 *True – they were treated as one person so people did not use their individual names.*
6 *True – this is probably why people always tried to give them the same things.*
7 *False – they made each other worse, for example at the dentist's.*
8 *True – their children also say that their voices and mannerisms are the same.*

4

Ask students to work in pairs to speculate about Clive and Keith Owen. Remind them not to look at the article at this stage. Quickly ask several pairs for their opinions. Then ask the class to read the article to find if they were right.

5

Ask students to read the article again and work with a partner to answer the questions.

You may want to ask students to do Exercise 4 from practice page 90. There is a lot of information in the article and students will need time to digest the contents.

Answers

1 *Telephone maintenance.*
2 *'Have I been drinking?' They are so alike that people cannot believe that they are seeing two people.*
3 *His brother Clive had had a car accident and broken some ribs. Keith felt the pain in his ribs as he was going to visit Clive in hospital.*
4 *Their mouths. They had both had stitches in the same part of their mouths.*

6

Play the cassette through and ask students to work in pairs to fill in the table.

Answers

1932	*twins born in Wales*
1947	*left school and worked together in hotel management in Bournemouth and the Lake District*
1950	*conscripted into the army*
1952	*joined the merchant navy (but they were not allowed to work on the same ship)*
1958	*met Georgia in a London street (Clive married her.)*

This would be a suitable place in which to introduce the language focus. Refer students to Language Summary 1 on practice page 90. Then ask them to do Exercises 1 and 2.

7

Ask students to discuss in groups of three.
Tell them that you will listen for their use of both, either, etc. During feedback ask for sentences using the grammar point.

Possible answers

There is no correct answer here but suggestions may include:
Clive and Keith had a happy childhood and a good relationship with their parents. Pauline doesn't talk specifically about this, but obviously disliked the way they were treated.

8

This would be a suitable place to introduce the second language focus, because it has direct relevance to this activity. Ask students to mingle to find their group. Within the groups ask them to work in pairs or fours to discuss the questions. Ask them to join with someone from another group to compare findings.
Make sure that everyone takes notes because they will need them for their homework.

Homework

Prepare by asking several pairs to report back, following the interview.
Ask students to give you answers using the grammar points from language focus 1 and 2 when appropriate.
Elicit headings to be included in the writing. After this students may need to go back to their partner to ask more questions.

Practice *page 90*

1

Ask students to do this exercise with a partner.

Answers

3 *either*	**4** *both*	**5** *Neither of*
6 *both of*	**7** *both*	**8** *Neither*
9 *either, both*	**10** *both, neither of*	**11** *both*

2

Students should do this exercise alone, and then discuss and correct their sentences with a partner.
This is a free activity, but possible answers might be:
Neither of us likes swimming.
We both take size 39 shoes.
The headmaster asked if either of us wanted to go on the school trip.

Language Summary 2

You may need to go through this carefully, as some students get confused when they have to agree with a negative statement.

3

Students can either do the exercise on their own, or work with a partner, taking it in turns to make the statement and the agreement.

Answers

3 *Neither have I.*	**7** *Neither would I.*
4 *Neither can I.*	**8** *Neither had I.*
5 *So do I.*	**9** *So do I.*
6 *So did I.*	**10** *So would I.*

4

Students should try to do this exercise on their own, and check their answers with a partner or with the whole class. You could make it into a competition, to see who can find the most correct answers in the shortest time.

1 *maintenance*	**2** *simultaneously*	**3** *pub*	**4** *set off*
5 *very hard*	**6** *choreographed*	**7** *tonsils*	**8** *stitches*

Lesson 2 *If you could choose*

Aims: to study a poem and to look at the expectations society has about the role of men and women.

Language focus

Second conditional

If you **could** live your life again, **would** you prefer to be a man or a woman?

Skills focus

- **Listening** to a poem and to short monologues for the main idea and for detail
- **Speaking:** comparing attitudes to men and women in the students' country or countries; discussion of statements about the role of men and women in society

Vocabulary focus

- Adjectives to describe people: *active, aggressive, brave, clever, clinging, emotional, gentle, handsome, kind, logical, overpowering, powerful, pretty, quiet, rational, ruthless, small, soft, strong, tall, tender, weak*
- Vocabulary in poem: *jet plane, gun, human nature, vicious, hussy, bawling, topsy-turvy, prams, cissy, left hook*
- Vocabulary for discussion: *biological make-up, equal opportunities, housework, upbringing*

Review

This gives practice in finding words efficiently in the dictionary. Dictate or write up words from the previous lesson that students did not know before, eg the vocabulary from Exercise 4 of practice page 90, *maintenance, choreographed, tonsils, pub, stitches*.
Make sure each pair has a dictionary. Ask them to find each word in the dictionary as quickly as they can and write down the number of the page where it appears.

Warmer

Write on the board:
Being young is . . . or, *Being male is . . . /Being female is . . .*
If you choose the latter, ask the class to work in single sex pairs. Elicit ideas to finish the sentence. Write all the ideas on the board.
Ask students to work in pairs to choose four of the ideas, put them in order and add a final line to finish the poem. The final [line] does not have to begin with Being young/male/female

One group produced this example:
Being male is playing football on Saturday afternoons.
Being male is going out to work every day.
Being male is not crying.
Being male is wearing trousers all the time, even though girls can wear dresses or trousers

1

If a lot of the vocabulary is new for the students it would be useful to do Exercise 4 from practice page 91.
Ask several pairs to read out their choices to the class.

2

Ask students to work in pairs to look at the chorus of the poem. Ask some pairs to tell the class their ideas. Write ideas for the rest of the poem on the board to check later.

3

Before playing the cassette through, check that students understand the vocabulary.
▭ Play the cassette once and ask students to compare their answers in pairs.

Answers

These are the words which are in the poem:
dirty, dolly, Janie, jet plane, noisy, Peter, pretty, screaming, sister, trouble

4

▭ Ask the girls to listen for Janie and the boys for Peter. Play the cassette through once and get boys to pair with girls to exchange information and opinions.

Answers

Janie: She is Peter's pretty sister who likes playing with dolls and copying her mother. She doesn't get dirty and is usually quiet.
Peter: is naughty (a terror), always running around imitating aeroplanes, pretending to be a cowboy and shooting at the neighbours. He's usually in trouble because he has done something he shouldn't do.

5 and 6

▭ Play the cassette through once. Ask the students to compare answers in pairs.
Before asking them to discuss what has happened you will probably find it useful to do Activity 6, the vocabulary exercise. Students may need dictionaries for this.

Answers 5

nasty, body, eye, cry, must, must, football, pushing, guilty, Doctor, Doctor

Answers 6

1 *come over* 2 *left hook* 3 *vicious* 4 *bawling*
5 *topsy-turvy* 6 *hussy* 7 *cissy*

7

Ask students to work in groups of six. However if you have students who find it difficult to speak in discussions, put the class in two circles, one facing in and one out, so that everyone has a partner from the other circle.

Ask the pairs to discuss the questions and then move the outside circle round so that everyone talks to a new partner. Help them by suggesting they talk first about people they know and then give their own opinions.

Repeat this three or four times.

Finish with a show of hands for and against each statement. Monitor for errors during the discussion and write them on the board for students to correct in pairs.

8

This would be an appropriate time to introduce the language focus. Refer students to the Language Summary on practice page 91, and then ask them to do Exercises 1 and 2.

▭ Play the cassette through once. Ask the class to answer the M/F questions.

Play the cassette again and ask students to work in pairs to compare their notes. Then they answer the question themselves.

Get responses from round the class asking students to use the second conditional where appropriate.

Answers

Name	M/F	Why?
Kerry	F	*Men can't have babies. Men can't cope on their own.*
Rob	F	*To experience situations from a female point of view. To see if men and society treat women badly, as some say. To see how men's and women's psychology differs.*
Paula	F	*Men hide their feelings and she doesn't like that. English men find it difficult to say 'I love you'. She'd like to be a man for a short time to find out what it's really like.*
Yves	M	*He enjoys being a man, doesn't know what women are like.*

9

Students stay in the same pairs to talk about these questions. They then form groups of six to exchange information. Several groups report back so as to share as many views as possible.

Homework

Students will probably have to ask the questions in their own language (although encourage them to find English speakers), which is all right as long as they write the answers in English and they report to the class in English.

Practice *page 91*

1 and 2

Refer students to the Language Summary. Then ask them to work alone to answer Exercise 1 and think about their own answers to the questions.

Next, in pairs, ask them to take it in turns to ask each other the questions.

Finish by getting students to write their answers down.

Answers 1

2 *didn't have, would you do*
3 *came from, would your life be,* or, *had come, would your life have been*
4 *were, would there be*
5 *could live, would you change*
6 *had, would you choose*
7 *were, would you do*

3

Ask a student to demonstrate these sounds if they can. Don't ask everyone to try at the same time!

Ask students to work in pairs to find the meanings of the words with a dictionary, and to write the sentences.

Ask them to add one more way of speaking, eg: *murmur, mutter, mumble, shriek.*

Individual students report back to the class. Ask them to say their sentence using the sound that they are describing.

4

Let students use dictionaries to find the stress patterns. Give one pair the words on cards and ask them to stick them on the board in the appropriate columns.

Use their answers when you go over the activity with the class. Drill the words if necessary.

Answers

■	■■	■■■	■■■■
brave	*clever*	*beautiful*	*emotional*
strong	*gentle*	*logical*	
weak	*handsome*	*powerful*	
	quiet	*rational*	
	ruthless		

5

Use this exercise as a revision of the vocabulary. You may like to start the next lesson with it.

Ask students to work alone to complete the sentences and to do so without using a dictionary.

Answers

2 *handsome* 3 *powerful* 4 *emotional* 5 *brave, beautiful*

Lesson 3 *Trading places*

Aim: to learn about what it is like to be someone else for a day.

Language focus

1 Conditional sentences without *if*
  Tell each other who you **would** be.

2 Conditional sentences with other words
  Unless I put my belt on my hips instead of my waist,
    I wouldn't look aggressive.
  As long as I wore men's clothes, people would treat me
    differently.

Skills focus

- **Listening** for detail of how someone spent a day
- **Speaking:** talking about an imaginary situation
- **Writing** about an imaginary day

Vocabulary focus

- Vocabulary from listening: *lipstick, unisex, a barber, sonny, a sponsor*
- Phrasal verbs – relationships: *get on with, go out with, grow apart, put up with, settle down, split up*
- Money raising: *charities, Comic Relief, cancer research, research centre, target, events, persuasiveness, persuade, publicity campaign*

Review

Display the tables from the Unit 9 Lesson 2 homework on the walls. Ask students to read and compare them. Find how many people wanted to change to the other sex.

Warmer

You may like to use Activity 1 as the warmer as this introduces the idea of disguise.

Or

Write on the board words that students may need help with, from the reading text in Activity 2 of this lesson. Write the words with the letters in the wrong order. Tell the students that they are all to do with raising money for something: *iyrhcta(charity); ecnarc (cancer); hrsceera (research); rgteat (target); tbpylciiu (publicity).*

1

Language Summary 2 and Exercise 3 on practice page 92 would fit in very well here as the language is directly relevant to the next activity.
Ask students to work in pairs to decide what the objects are.
Do the first one with the class and elicit appropriate language

for the activity. Write the phrases on the board. For example: *It looks like . . . , It looks as if . . . , It might be . . . , Do you think it could be . . . , Perhaps it's . . . , What do you think it could be? No, I don't think so.*

Answers

headphones from a personal stereo, a dartboard, a camera, a compact disc

2

If students haven't looked at the definition, elicit the word disguise. Otherwise ask students to study the definition and ask them to give examples of why someone would go in disguise. Students will need to scan the article alone and then work with a partner to compare their ideas. Remind students that they do not need to understand every word but just find out what the disguise is.

Answers

People can choose to be somebody else for one day, and dress to look like the other person.

3

Give students time to read the text carefully and then work with a partner to answer the questions.

Answers

1 *When her mother-in-law was told she had cancer Fiona felt that the doctor did not know enough about why she had developed the disease.*
2 *To build a cancer research centre.*
3 *£15 million, but she hopes she will get more.*
4 *Persuading people to give money to charities.*
5 *Members of the public and celebrities.*

4

Students will probably need dictionaries but ask them to work in pairs to help each other first.

Answers

| 1 *b* | 2 *e* | 3 *a* | 4 *c* | 5 *d* |

5

Prepare students by having a very short brainstorm about the three questions.
Ask students to work in pairs to discuss them. Then several pairs report back to the class.

6

Play the cassette through once for students to compare their ideas with what really happened.
Get answers from a couple of students to see if they were correct. Play the cassette again for students to complete the table. Ask students to compare answers with a partner.

Answers

clothes *bought a dark suit, raincoat, pair of heavy work boots*
hair *went to barber's, cut her hair very short around the ears*
face *make-up artist put dark make up around her chin*
general physical appearance *moved belt to hips to look more aggressive*

7

📼 Play the rest of the cassette through. Ask students to complete the table and then compare answers with a partner.

Answers

in the street	*policeman called her 'sonny'; she felt invisible*
in the men's club	*no problem, treated wonderfully, waiter brought her drinks, everyone called her 'Sir'*
in the pub	*got to the bar easily, usually women can't get near the bar*
walking home	*felt safe to walk through park, bought lipstick to remind herself that she really was a woman*

8

This would be a suitable place to introduce Language Summary 1 on practice page 92. Exercises 1 and 2 would fit in well here. The students would then be able to use the language during this discussion activity.
Ask the students to work in pairs to discuss the questions. Tell them that they should be prepared to tell another pair their ideas. Give pairs five minutes to talk. Then ask pairs to form fours and exchange ideas. Ask several groups to report to the class.

9 and Homework

Prepare for this activity and also for the homework by asking for the name of a well-known person. Ask what clothes you would need if you were to impersonate that person, and what you would have to do during the day and so on.
Give students time to think about this alone and make notes before they work in groups.
Ask students to suggest problems and things which might happen as they listen to each other.
Agree on the length of the paragraph. Tell students that they can illustrate it with pictures of their person.

Practice *page 92*

Language Summary 1

Make sure students understand that we leave out *if* clauses if the condition is understood in the situation. Therefore in the example 'Tell each other who you would be' we do not have to add 'if you were trading places for the day'. This has been made clear to everyone during the lesson.

1

Ask students to do Exercise 1 alone. Then in pairs they take it in turns to ask and answer the questions.

Possible answers

2 *I would try to find a policeman. I would follow them and stop them.*
3 *I would go to my embassy. I would phone my parents and ask them to send me more money.*
4 *I would say no. I would ask them why they wanted the money.*

2

Refer students to Language Summary 1 and get them to work in pairs to do the exercise.

Answers

3 *As long as* or *If*	4 *If*	5 *Unless*
6 *If*	7 *As long as* or *If*	8 *Unless*

3

Ask students to do this exercise in pairs.
To extend the activity, bring in some obscure pictures for students to speculate about, as in Lesson 3 Activity 1.

Answers

What a lovely shirt! It feels like silk.
The girl in black looks like someone I know.
I don't know what it is. It looks like a tool for cutting.
This pie tastes delicious.
Ric and Kio seem really happy together.
What an old cassette! It sounds like something from the 60s.
Deren seems like the right man for the job.
Cars and lorries look too big in these narrow streets.

4

Go through the stages of a relationship and match each phrasal verb to a stage:
– the meeting: *get on with*
– the courtship: *go out with*
– marriage: *settle down, put up with*
– having children: *look after, put up with*
– divorce: *grow apart, split up*
Ask students to work alone to do the exercise. Remind them that they may have to change the tense of the verbs.

Answers

2 *go out with*	3 *settle down*	4 *grew apart*
5 *look after*	6 *put up with*	7 *split up*

Extend the activity by asking students to make a word map under the main heading of relationships.
Brainstorm sub-headings – *wedding, marriage, courtship, engagement* etc.

The theme of this unit is environmental issues.

Lesson 1 *Green is the colour*

Aim: to introduce environmental issues as a topic.

Language focus

Future with *will* and *going to*
Buy recycled products : this **will** encourage manufacturers to supply them.
What is Hong Kong **going to** do about this problem?

Skills focus

- **Reading:** using information to complete a text
- **Writing:** making a poster
- **Speaking:** describing a problem
- **Listening** for specific information

Vocabulary focus

- Colour: *green, emerald green, sea green, dark green, light green, sage green, pale green*
- Pollution: *carbon monoxide, chemicals, fumes, industrial waste, pollutant, rubbish, sewage plant, smog, toxic gases, traffic, ozone layer, factory*

Review

Ask students to read their day as someone else (homework for Unit 9 Lesson 3) to each other.
Find out the different people students have chosen to be. If one or two celebrities were very popular, you could find out why, and see whether different students had them doing similar things.

1

Activity 1 is a warmer. It introduces the idea of green having more connotations than the colour alone.
Ask students to work in pairs to answer the questions.
Write the colours on the board and ask several students for their answers to the other questions.

Answers

Possible colours are: *dark green, pale green, light green, emerald green, sea green, sage green, moss green, lime green*

2

Before doing this activity, check the meanings with the class.
Also practise pronunciation, drilling words if necessary.
Practice page 93 Exercise 3 would fit in well here.
Ask students to work in pairs to check the meaning of the words, using dictionaries if necessary.
Ask students to write the words beside the appropriate pictures.

When they have finished join pairs together to compare their work.
Ask one group for their answers to one picture, another group for the second picture, and a third for the third picture.

Possible answers

Picture 1: *photo of a waste pipe*
Picture 2: *photo of rubbish dump*
Picture 3: *photo of a traffic jam*

3

This listening passage is a pattern for the students for Activity 5 when they are required to talk about a problem in their country.
▣ Play the cassette through once. Ask students to work alone and decide on the picture and tick the words.
Ask students to compare their answers.

Answers

The picture Larry is talking about is on the bottom left of the page.

The words Larry used are: *pollutants, factories, pollution, rivers, sewage plant*

4

▣ Play the cassette through again and ask students to work together to answer the questions.

Answers

1 *pollutants from factories around Hong Kong; pollution from the population of Hong Kong; polluted rivers which flow into the harbour*
2 *The government is going to build a new sewage plant to treat the sewage before it gets to the harbour.*

The Language Summary on practice page 93 would fit in here as the relevant language appears on the cassette. They can also do Exercises 1 and 2.

5

This gives practice with the language point.
Discuss the structure of Larry's talk: he states the problem, the reasons and what the government is doing and is going to do.
Give students a few minutes to think about what they are going to say, but do not let them write any notes.
You may like to ask students to speak for one minute only, without hesitating.
Ask the listener to listen for three items of information. Go very quickly round the class getting this information.
Then change the roles. Find out if everyone agrees with what has been said.

6

Ask students to work with a partner to do this. Make it into a competition. Students put their hands up when they have found the answers.

Answers

The answers given depend on what individual students do to help the environment.

7

Ask students to work in pairs to do this exercise. Check the answers by asking individual students to read out sentences.

Answers

1 *harmful*
2 *packaging*
3 *manufacturer*
4 *carbon dioxide or acid rain*
5 *energy-saving, switching off*
6 *paper, glass, metal, recycling point*
7 *Recycling*

8

Ask students to work in groups of four.
Prepare for the activity by eliciting what makes a poster attractive, eye-catching, memorable. (Remind them of the work they did in Unit 3 Lesson 3 on advertisements.)
Tell students that everyone needs to take notes as they will need them for their homework.

Homework

Tell students to use A4 paper or card and to use coloured pens.

Practice *page 93*

Language Summary

▭ Play the cassette from Lesson 1 Activities 3–4 again. Ask students to listen for the language Larry uses to tell us about his government's intentions for the future.
Refer students to the Language Summary.

1 and 2

Ask the students to do Exercises 1 and 2 with a partner. Check the answers round the class.

Answers 1

1 *will die*   2 *are you going to do*   3 *am going to*
4 *will go*   5 *will have to*   6 *am going to*
7 *is going to*

Answers 2

1 *B: 'm going to put*   2 *B: will start*
3 *B: will take*   4 *A: am going to use*
                            B: will go

Give more practice in using *going to* by asking all students to write the following sentence at the top of a sheet of paper:
What are you going to do after the lesson?

Ask them to pass the paper to a neighbour, who adds an answer, comment or further question and then passes it to someone else. All the writing is visible all the time.
After about four to five rounds students can read the papers.

3

Ask students to work in pairs to mark the stress on the words. They may need to use a dictionary.
Drill the words and use the opportunity to revise meanings.
Demonstrate weak forms and schwa /ə/ by writing a sentence such as *I want a cup of tea*.
Demonstrate that we do not say *a* and *of* in their strong form.
We stress words that give us information. Elicit the type of words: main verbs, adjectives, nouns, adverbs, etc.
Do a couple of the words in the exercise with the class. Ask students to work in pairs to mark the weak sound. Encourage them to try to say the words.
Get feedback by drilling the vocabulary.

Answers

*appli**a**nces*	*biodegr**a**dable*	*car**bon** dioxide*
*carrier **bags***	*chem**i**cals*	*con**tainers***
*dis**pos**able*	*in**dus**trial*	*ozone **layer***
pollution	*recycled*	*un**lea**ded **pet**rol*

/ə/ /ə/	/ə/	/ə/
*appli**a**nces*	*biodegrad**a**ble*	*carb**o**n dioxide*
/ə/	/ə/	/ə/ /ə/
*carri**e**r bags*	*chemic**a**ls*	*cont**a**iners*
/ə/	/ə/	/ə/
*dispos**a**ble*	*industri**a**l*	*ozone lay**e**r*
/ə/ /ə/	/ə/	/ə/
*poll**u**tion*	*recycl**e**d*	*unleaded petr**o**l*

4

This exercise uses some of the vocabulary from Activity 7 and Exercise 3. Ask students to work with a partner.

Answers

2 *Diana didn't know that the aerosol sprays she used were damaging the ozone layer.*
3 *Jairo found out that one person generates three tonnes of carbon dioxide per year.*
4 *They both decided to do four things each to help.*
5 *They now recycle glass, metals and paper.*
6 *They don't buy products which have unnecessary packaging.*
7 *They use low-energy light bulbs and turn off unused electrical appliances.*

Lesson 2 *The greenest school in Britain*

Aim: for students to consider ways of helping the environment around them.

Language focus

1 Revision of passives
Everything **is collected** and **reused**.
They looked at the way stationery **was used**.

2 Purpose clauses
The school has its own garden **so that** they can learn about the environment.

Skills focus

- **Reading** a quiz and reading an article for specific information
- **Listening** to children talking about their school
- **Writing** a formal letter or memo about environmental issues

Vocabulary focus

- Objects in quiz: *greens, cabbage, emerald, avocado, calories, records, greenfly, coaches, frog*
- From text: *dripping, bin liner, ozone-unfriendly, stationery, scrutinised, of their own accord*
- Recycled items: *banana skin, bottle top, recycled paper towels, aluminium, fabric, rubbish bags*

Review

Display round the walls the posters that students have made about the environment (homework for Unit 10 Lesson 1). Students vote for the best one and discuss why it is the best.

Warmer

Write one of these well-known idioms on the board. Discuss its meaning, and compare it with similar or contrasting idioms from the students' own culture.
Then write up two more and ask students to work with a partner to discuss the meanings.
to have green fingers (to be very good at making plants grow)
to be green with envy (jealous)
green belt (an area of land that is protected from development)
to be green (this has two meanings: *to be naïve* and *to be environmentally conscious*)

1

This is a competition, so do not let the students open their books until you are ready to start.

Ask students to work in groups of four. Tell them that when you give a starting signal they are to answer the questions as quickly as possible. As soon as they have finished they should put up their hands.
When this happens stop everyone and check the answers with the group who finished first.

Answers

1 *Richard Burton*
2 *Green Card*
3 *1981*
4 *New South Wales, Australia*
5 *Brazil*
6 *Bartley Green, near Birmingham*
7 *avocado*
8 *Kermit*
9 *phone card*
10 *The Body Shop*

2

Keep the students in their groups of four. Ask each group to elect a secretary to record the ideas and to report them to the rest of the class.

Possible answers

use recycled paper
always write on both sides of the paper
recycle as much as possible, eg bottles, cans, bottle tops
don't buy food which is packaged

3

This reading is for gist, therefore before they read remind the students that they do not need to understand every word.
Ask students to work in their groups to compare their ideas with those in the text.
During the feedback elicit all the ideas mentioned in the text.

Answers

switching unused lights off
checking if taps are dripping
no waste, everything is recycled or reused
don't use ozone-unfriendly appliances
be careful with photocopying
come to school in cars which use unleaded petrol
more children brought to school in fewer cars
towels made of recycled paper
stop bringing wrapped snacks such as chocolate and crisps
grow own vegetables and herbs
play area made from recycled things
take their rubbish home
made posters to encourage everyone

4

Ask students to read the text carefully and work in their groups to help each other with the meaning of the words. Only allow the use of dictionaries as a last resort.

Answers

1 *d* 2 *e* 3 *b* 4 *f* 5 *a* 6 *c*

5

🔊 Before you play the cassette, tell the students that they will hear the children speaking in the order given in Activity 5. Ask them to work alone to circle the paragraphs. They then compare their answers with a partner.

Answers

Stephanie: para 8   Steven: para 7
Alice: para 9   Paul: para 6

6

🔊 Play the cassette through again and ask students to work alone to find the answers.

Answers

1 Bring lunch in a box, not in plastic bags, so you can use it every day.
2 Help animals in the wild, for example, feed the birds in winter.
3 Give up smoking because it's bad for the ozone layer and the packaging creates rubbish.
4 Use pens that can be refilled.

7

If students are interested they could start a project like the one in this lesson. Get them to work in their groups to add more ideas and to decide what they feel they could do to help the environment. Ask each group to present their ideas. Then decide as a class which you are going to try.

Homework

Prepare students by eliciting how to lay out a letter, including suitable greetings and endings. Use the proposals from Activity 7 in the letter.
Tell students that the letter you believe to be the best will be given to the School Principal for him or her to consider adopting the proposals in the school.

Practice *page 94*

Language Summary 1

This is a revision of the passive.
Ask the students, in pairs, to write a sentence in the passive and to discuss how the passive is made and when it is used. Focus on how the passive tells us about the agent. Note that sometimes the agent is implied.
Ask a pair to write their sentence on the board and explain why it is in the passive.
Ask students to find two sentences in the text in Lesson 2 Activity 3 that are in the passive.

1

Ask the students to do this exercise in pairs.

Answers

2 The school sends many things to be recycled.
3 The children looked at how staff and students used stationery.
4 Everyone wasted food.
5 The teachers replaced paper towels with recycled paper.
6 The children found out about how much rubbish they created.

2

This gives practice in changing the active to the passive. Ask students to work with a partner to answer the questions.

Answers

2 Far too many new cars which weren't energy-efficient were bought.
3 Too much packaging is used.
4 Too many pre-packed foods are used by my family.
5 Too many disposable products are bought by nearly half my school.
6 Less electricity and environmentally harmful products were used in the past.

3

Refer students to Language Summary 2 and do several of the questions together.
Then ask students to work in pairs to answer the questions.

Answers

2 The children gave up eating sweets so that they could throw away less plastic rubbish./In order to throw away less plastic rubbish, the children gave up eating sweets.
3 The teachers used fewer photocopies in order to save a lot of paper./The teachers used fewer photocopies so that they could save a lot of paper.
4 In order to use fewer cars the parents shared them./So that they could use fewer cars the parents shared them.
5 In order to cut down on rubbish and pollution, Steven's dad gave up smoking./Steven's dad gave up smoking so that he could cut down on rubbish and pollution.
6 The children decided to use solar calculators in order to avoid wasting batteries./The children decided to use solar calculators so that they could avoid wasting batteries.
7 In order to stop destroying the ozone layer, the cleaner used environmentally-friendly products./The cleaner used environmentally-friendly products so that she could stop destroying the ozone layer.
8 The teachers bought board markers which they could refill so that they could throw away fewer pens./The teachers bought board markers which they could refill in order to throw away fewer pens.

Lesson 3 *The techno-solution*

Aim: to talk about possible solutions to some environmental problems.

Language focus

Future predictions and possibilities
Planes **would** release dust which **would** keep the sunlight out.
Americans **may** find that hard to accept.
No one knows what dust **might** do.
Trying to control climates **could** also cause political problems.

Skills focus

- **Reading** a magazine article to take notes
- **Speaking:** describing a solution to a problem; having a discussion
- **Writing:** designing a cartoon and writing a caption

Vocabulary focus

- Techno-solutions: *geo-engineering, dust, soot, shoot, metal-coated hydrogen-filled balloons, orbit, mirrors, climates, dams*
- Problems: *drought, flood, heat waves, killer storms*
- Space: *atmosphere, stratosphere, orbit, ozone layer, greenhouse effect*

Review

Display the letters from the homework in Unit 10 Lesson 2 around the walls and ask the students to walk round in pairs and correct any mistakes of layout and grammar.
After five minutes either tell the class which letter you have chosen for the School Principal or ask the students to vote.

Warmer

This introduces and practises *might* and *could* for predicting what something is.
Ask two students to stand with their backs to the board. They are the guessers. On the board write the name of a well-known object, eg: a pencil, a cup, a book. The guessers have to find out the name of the object you have written.
The class help the guessers by suggesting things they might/could do with the object. They should not give obvious information.

1

This activity gives more practice in using *might, may, could*.
Ask students to work in pairs to look at the pictures.
Encourage them to spend time thinking about it. Then ask them to compare their ideas with another pair.
Ask several pairs for their explanations.

2

Ask students to read the article to find out what the pictures are about. The text is fairly dense so tell students that they need to skim the article to find where the information is.
Ask some students to tell the class the meanings of the pictures. Find if any of the predictions were correct.

Answers

Top left:	*mirrors which deflect the sun's rays away from the earth and so cool it down.*
Bottom left:	*metal-coated balloons float into space to reflect sunlight.*
Top right:	*passenger aeroplanes release dust and soot to keep sunlight away from earth.*
Bottom right:	*guns from navy ships fire dust and soot into space.*

3

Ask students to work in pairs to match words from the text with their definitions. They may need to use dictionaries.
You may want to ask students to choose another three or four words from the text which they do not know the meaning of.

Answers

1 *a*   2 *b*   3 *a*   4 *a*   5 *a*

4

Give students time to read the article carefully. Ask them to work alone to write notes.

Answers

Advantages of techno-solutions
You don't have to change things you do every day.
We could continue to burn coal and oil without all the bad effects like drought, floods, heatwaves, storms.
Disadvantages of techno-solutions
They would be very expensive.
No one knows if techno-solutions will cause more problems.
Once you use one solution you may need another.
Climate control could cause political problems: which country would decide to release the dust?

This would be a suitable place to introduce the Language Summary on practice page 95 for future predictions and possibilities. Students could then do Exercises 1 and 2.

5

Ask students to compare their answers in groups of four and discuss the two questions. Ask groups to choose a spokesperson for their group.
Each group reports back to the class with the advantages and disadvantages.

6

Give groups large sheets of paper to present their solution on. Keep a strict time limit and remind students after five minutes and when there are two minutes to go. If there is time and the size of the class permits, get each group to come to the front of the class to present their solution. If that isn't possible, get one group to present their solution to another.
Monitor for errors during the activity, focusing particularly on the use of *will*, *might* and *may*.

Homework

Read the cartoon with the students and make sure they understand the meaning.
Prepare students by getting them to work in pairs to discuss ideas before working on their own at home.
N.B. The caption for the last picture in the cartoon is, 'Is this any way to treat your mother?' Ask the students to write it in their books.

Practice *page 95*

Language Summary

Refer students to Lesson 3 Activity 5 as the language they use for this is directly related to the Language Summary.

1

Refer students to the Language Summary and ask them to do Exercise 1 with a partner.

Answers

2 *The hole in the ozone layer might not grow any bigger.*
3 *People could be more aware of environmental problems.*
4 *We may still have time to save the planet.*
5 *In the future companies may use more recycled products in packaging.*
6 *People might buy more energy-efficient cars and not just the fastest ones available.*
7 *Some people could still be unaware of environmental dangers.*
8 *Governments in the future could ban cars.*
9 *Carbon monoxide and methane gas levels might decrease.*

2

This gives more practice in predicting and speculating and is directly related to Lesson 3 Activities 2 and 5.
Ask students to do Exercise 2 alone and to compare their sentences with a partner.

Possible answers

2 *He will kill himself. He might jump.*
3 *There could have been an accident. Everyone will be late for work today.*
4 *The balloons may reflect the sun's rays. This method will cost a lot of money.*

3

Ask students to do this in pairs. Check the answers with the whole class.
Depending on the mistakes made, revise the necessary prepositions.

Answers

2 *in*	3 *During*	4 *At*	5 *for*	6 *until*
7 *After*	8 *By*	9 *for*	10 *on*	

Section 1: Comprehension
[20 marks]

Most people probably associate the Japanese with hard work – and they do work hard. However, they also know how to enjoy themselves. Today's leisure industry, as in other countries around the world, is big business.

Just as people around the world love Japanese activities such as *karaoke*, many Japanese people enjoy hobbies from Europe and America. Baseball, which is so close to the hearts of the Japanese that they may not remember its American origin, is now the most popular spectator sport in Japan after sumo wrestling.

The traditional martial arts are popular participation sports. Judo, which became an Olympic sport in 1964, is the most popular, both at home and abroad. The popularity of karate, Aikido and Kendo is more recent. Golf, volleyball and tennis are also big in Japan but the number one free time activity (apart from watching TV) is *pachinko*. This is a game similar to pinball in which you have to place a ball in the right hole. Men and women of all ages play the machines in enormous arcades.

Theatre-lovers have a great choice in Japan. There are modern plays and two traditional types of drama. *Noh* plays were first performed in the 14th century; today about 240 *Noh* plays are performed on stage, in a style which is not much different from that of six centuries ago. There are usually only three roles in a *Noh* play, with female parts taken by masked male actors. The performance is accompanied by music which is played on instruments such as the *taiko* (a type of drum). *Kabuki*, a spectacular theatre form which developed in the 17th century, is much more popular among today's Japanese audiences; the majority, however, never see it except on television.

Japan is also the home of Nintendo and computer games. But as well as all the latest high-tech entertainment, there are many traditional pastimes which have been around for thousands of years. *Ikebana*, the skill of flower-arranging, has been popular for more than 1300 years. Kite-flying also dates back many centuries. *Shuji* or *shodo* (writing characters with a brush) is still considered a serious achievement; though with the increased availability of Japanese-language word processors, it may suffer a decline.

Everyone in Japan is completely crazy about comics, which they call *manga*. Adults read them just as much as children. There are comics on every subject you can possibly think of, from cooking to insurance plus plenty of action stories. The single most popular comic in Japan sells more than eight million copies every week!

1 a Read the article and think of a suitable title for it. Write the title below. [2 marks]

_____

b Are these sentences true (T) or false (F)? Write T or F in the box. [8 marks]

Example: *Karaoke* is Japanese in origin. [T]
1 Sumo wrestling is more popular than baseball.
2 Karate isn't as old or as popular as judo.
3 Volleyball is played in Japan.
4 You can only see traditional drama at Japanese theatres.
5 *Noh* plays have changed a lot over the years.
6 Most Japanese people have never seen *Kabuki* at the theatre.
7 Arranging flowers has been popular since 1300.
8 Eight million comics are sold every week.

c Write answers to these questions about the passage. You do not need to write sentences. [10 marks]

1 What is the most popular leisure activity in Japan?

_____

2 What is special about the actors in *Noh* plays?

_____

3 How long has kite-flying been popular in Japan?

_____

4 Why might *shuji* become less popular?

_____

5 Who buys and reads comics in Japan?

_____

Section 2: Communication
[20 marks]

2 a Write questions for these answers. [10 marks]

1 _____
Yes, I have, but I didn't understand it all.

2 _____
Mary does. She's got her own car.

3 _____
I've lived here all my life.

4 _____
She can't have done. Her swimming costume's on her bed.

5 _____
He started walking to work in order to get some exercise.

b Write sentences beginning with these words. [10 marks]

6 My mother warned me not _____

7 If you see Robert,_____

_____

8 When the accident happened,_____

_____

9 Although I have a lot of friends,_____

_____

10 If I had more money,_____

_____

Section 3: Language
[20 marks]

3 a Choose ten of these words to complete the first ten spaces in the conversation. Underline each word you choose. [10 marks]

Example: A being   B feeling   C looking

1 A been   B come   C gone

2 A at   B on   C since

3 A had   B has   C have

4 A if   B that   C to

5 A neither   B nor   C so

6 A couldn't   B mightn't   C mustn't

7 A best   B better   C good

8 A smoke   B smoked   C smoking

9 A enough   B more   C near

10 A could   B had   C would

b Complete the last ten spaces with your own words. Write one word in each space. [10 marks]

PETER: Hello, Margaret. You're _looking_ well.
MARGARET: Thanks, Peter. I've just (1) _____ back from holiday. I only got home (2) _____ Sunday.
PETER: You lucky thing! Where did you go?
MARGARET: I went to Italy for a skiing holiday. A friend of mine (3) _____ rented a flat for a week with some colleagues. She asked me (4) _____ I wanted to go with her. I had a great time and (5) _____ did my friend. I (6) _____ have enjoyed myself more! It was the (7) _____ holiday I've ever had! Nobody in the flat smoked, so I gave up (8) _____ too!
PETER: Well done!
MARGARET: A week wasn't long (9) _____ . If I (10) _____ have the time off work, I would go back again. But I'll go again next year.
PETER: You've lived in Italy, haven't you?
MARGARET: That's right. I (11) _____ to live in Milan. I worked there (12) _____ over two years.

That's when I (13) _____ to ski. We went to the mountains (14) _____ weekend in winter.
PETER: You (15) _____ be good at skiing!
MARGARET: Yes, my skiing's better than my Italian! You (16) _____ to try skiing, Peter.
PETER: Oh, I don't know. I'm (17) _____ old.
MARGARET: No, you're not. Most of the people (18) _____ were in the flat were much older than you. You (19) _____ have to be young to enjoy skiing.
PETER: Well, you never know. I (20) _____ go with you next year!

Section 4: Writing
[20 marks]

4   A friend has just written to you with a problem. Your friend wants to spend a year travelling around the world when he/she finishes university. Your friend's parents want him/her to stay at home and get a job instead. Write a letter to your friend giving advice.

Dear _____

_____

_____

_____

_____

_____

_____

_____

_____

_____

_____

To the Teacher

Each of the four levels of Accelerate is accompanied by a test, which consists of:

- a *To the teacher* section
- photocopiable worksheets for students
- an answer key

The tests can serve two purposes.

1 Diagnostic. The tests can be used to enable the teacher to assess the level of a class as a whole and to identify general areas of weakness before students begin the course.

2 Achievement. The tests can be used to allow both students and teacher to identify progress made during the course. Students can repeat the test upon completion of their course even if they have already taken the same test at the beginning; in this way they can assess their improvement.

Each test is divided into six parts. These are:

1 Comprehension
2 Communication
3 Language
4 Writing
5 Dictation (optional)
6 Oral task (optional)

Each section of the test carries 20 marks. The marks can be adjusted by the teacher, with greater or less emphasis given to particular sections.

Optional section 5: Dictation
[20 marks]

Tell students that you are going to dictate five sentences. Explain that you will read each sentence three times. First, read each sentence at normal speed. Then read the sentences slowly, breaking them up into phrases. Finally, read the sentences once more at normal speed.

4 marks for each sentence. Deduct one mark for each mistake.

1 You can invite either of the children.
2 I'll never get used to living in the country.
3 I bought some shoes that were the wrong colour.
4 Our luggage was searched before we got our tickets.
5 Those women look as if they get on really well together.

Optional section 6: Speaking task [20 marks]

Students work in pairs. Give each student a copy of the task. If possible, try to record each conversation so that you can assess students' work at a later point in time.

Tell students what you will take into consideration when assessing their oral work. Criteria should include:

- fluency: speaking without too much hesitation (4 marks)

- grammatical accuracy: speaking without too many mistakes (4 marks)

- pronunciation: making individual sounds correctly, using stress, rhythm and intonation appropriately (4 marks)

- vocabulary: using a wide range of appropriate vocabulary (4 marks)

- communication: being able to ask questions, give opinions/advice etc (4 marks)

Speaking Task

If you could live your life again, what would you change? Be prepared to tell your partner about your life now, what changes you would make and why.

Work with your partner. Find out what changes your partner would make and why. If you were your partner, would you make the same changes or would you make others?

Section 1: Comprehension
[20 marks]

1 a 2 marks: suggestions include:

Free time activities in Japan
Free time Japanese-style
Traditional and modern activities in Japan

b 8 marks: 1 mark for each correct answer.

1 T   2 T   3 T   4 F
5 F   6 T   7 F   8 F

c 10 marks: 2 marks for each correct answer. Answers can be in note form rather than in complete sentences. Suggestions include:

1 watching TV
2 usually three male actors
3 for many centuries
4 because Japanese-language word processors are now available
5 adults and children

Section 2: Communication
[20 marks]

2 a 10 marks: 2 marks for each question. Deduct one mark for each mistake. Any correct question is acceptable. Suggestions include:

1 Have you ever seen an English film/read a French magazine?
2 Who drives to work?
3 How long have you lived here?
4 Has she/Mary gone swimming?
5 Why did he/James start walking to work?

b 10 marks: 2 marks for each sentence. Deduce one mark for each mistake. Any correct sentence completion is acceptable. Suggestions include:

6 My mother warned me not to get home late.
7 If you see Robert, can you ask him to phone me?
8 When the accident happened, I was going into the supermarket.
9 Although I have a lot of friends, I don't go out very often.
10 If I had more money, I would buy a larger flat.

Section 3: Language
[20 marks]

3 a 10 marks: 1 mark for each correct answer.

1 B   2 B   3 A   4 A   5 C
6 A   7 A   8 C   9 A   10 B

b 10 marks: 1 mark for each appropriate answer. Suggestions include:

11 used
12 for
13 learned/began/started
14 every
15 must
16 ought/have
17 too/very
18 who
19 don't
20 may/might/could

Section 4: Writing
[20 marks]

You might like to tell students what you will take into consideration when marking their written work. Criteria should include:

- efficient communication of meaning (7 marks)
- grammatical accuracy (7 marks)
- coherence in the ordering of the information or ideas (3 marks)
- capitalisation and punctuation (3 marks)

It is probably better not to use a rigid marking system with the written part of the test. If, for example, you always deduct a mark for a grammatical mistake, you may find that you are over-penalising students who write a lot or who take risks. Deduct marks if students haven't written the minimum number of sentences stated in the test.

Unit 1, Lesson 1, Activities 4 and 5

1

Well, my name is Abdullah. I come from Yemen and er … I study English in England. Here I have a lot of opportunity to improve my English. In my free time I go to meet people in the street and in pubs. I watch TV a lot, and listen to the radio too, and I um … like listening to songs and reading er … the words at the same time and I … er … try to discuss the meaning of the words with my English friends. I like travelling, so in England I see lots of different cities and visit museums and exhibitions, so I'm very lucky to be here.

2

Well, my name is Reza. I'm from Persia, which now they call Iran, and I'm studying in England. Er … I've been here about 3 years. To improve my English most of the time what I do I record my own voice on cassette, ask questions and then listen and answer. Another thing I do is I watch English films sometimes and also I listen to lots of songs and they both improve my vocabulary and the words I don't know I look up in a dictionary. Since I came to England I haven't had a friend who speaks my language. That way I can learn English a lot quicker because I have to speak it all the time.

3

My name is Premi Mirchandane. I come from the south of Spain. To improve my English I sometimes read books and magazines in English, for example Newsweek Magazine. I also try to watch er … programmes on satellite TV and on Gibraltar Channel, which you can get where I live. I'm also working in an import-export office so I have to speak to clients in English, so I spend most of the time speaking English there. But er… really, going to class and working hard is enough for me.

4

My name is Osmantan Celebi from Turkey. In Turkey I go to an English course at weekends, but apart from the course I try to read in English about electronics because er… that's what I'm interested in. I also read instructions manuals in English, because I have a lot of electronic items and the manuals are always in English. I make lists of vocabulary to learn each day and pin them up on my wall. I also like watching satellite TV, so I watch the news and other interesting programmes on English TV. At first I found it difficult to understand, but after a while I got used to it.

Unit 1, Lesson 2, Activities 4 and 5

Well, before I went to Indonesia I thought I'd better learn some words in Indonesian. There was a girl who I knew who had been teaching there and spoke Indonesian and I asked her what sort of vocabulary I should learn. She wrote a list of useful words and phrases – things like what to say in shops, you know, how much does it cost, have you got any pens, things like that – and also words and phrases you need when you meet people. She said that one of the first things Indonesian people ask you is 'Are you married?' So I had to learn how to reply to that! I also learnt the words for fruit and vegetables, oh, and of course the numbers, so I could pay for things. Another friend, who was also going, helped because we decided to spend time together learning things – we practised repeating new words and managed to help each other.

Um …, ww… when I arrived, one of the first things that happened was my suitcase got lost on the flight, so I had to go to the lost property office in the airport and describe it. It was a large, square, blue nylon suitcase and inside it were my new brightly-coloured cotton clothes suitable for Indonesia. I hadn't learnt all these words, so I had to look them up and it took a long time. But I never forgot those words.

In my second week there, one of the other teachers and I decided to buy a car together. We had no problems with the car until one day when we went on a long trip to a small island. Well, we were driving along a very narrow road when suddenly the brakes failed. Well, fortunately I'm quite good with cars, so I knew what the problem was. We stopped at the side of the road and I took the back wheel off. Well, soon a whole crowd of very interested men and children had gathered round, all wanting to know what the problem was and how they could help. I tried very hard to explain, but I didn't know the special words for the parts of the car. I pointed at the parts and they told me the words. There were so many people that I had to tell the story lots of times – so again I learnt the words very quickly!

I think out of all the words I learnt before travelling to Indonesia, the numbers were the most useful because I used them all the time right from the first day. But the words I remembered easiest were how to describe things, my suitcase in particular, and how to talk about cars. I think it's when you're forced to use new words that you really remember them.

Unit 1, Lesson 2, Activity 5

I think out of all the words I learnt before travelling to Indonesia, the numbers were the most useful because I used them all the time right from the first day. But the words I remembered easiest were how to describe things, my suitcase in particular, and how to talk about cars. I think it's when you're forced to use new words that you really remember them.

Unit 1, Lesson 3, Activity 2

I was born in the Czech Republic and am now 45 years old. I came to study English in Cambridge when I was 18. I had started to learn English when I was only 16, but when I arrived I couldn't understand anyone and no one could understand me! While I was in Cambridge, I met Mike, an English undergraduate at the university, and I ended up marrying him. My two daughters, Adele, who is 21, and Klara, who is 20, are studying engineering, and were both born in England. However, when Adele was two years old, we went to live in Paris, France, where we still live today. When I first went to France I had great difficulty learning French and, because of these experiences in France, I was determined that both of my children would grow up speaking English, Czech and French.

Unit 2, Lesson 1, Activities 1 and 2

Well, I didn't actually choose my job, I sort of, um, gradually drifted into it. I started to help, um … a friend, who was teaching the Vietnamese boat people, you know, the… the Vietnamese who had to leave Vietnam and they came, well, all over the world, but some of them came to England and they had to learn English very quickly. I started to help a friend and I really enjoyed it. And, in fact, at the centre, they asked me er… would I do some teaching, and of course I said yes. But when I went into the classroom I soon found out I… it wasn't as easy as that and so I trained, and so I've been a teacher ever since.

Um … I think, though, that your character attracts you to certain, you know, to the right kind of job and so I think I have got quite a few of the characteristics that is, are needed for a teacher. I mean, I like being with people. I think people would say I was quite friendly, and course you're with people all the time, and I … love it, particularly with young people. Um … and although I'm not patient with my family, um, I'm actually patient with, like, everybody else, and I think you do need to be patient, um, when you're teaching.

I'm quite a lively person which is good, as well, because, um … , […] holds the students' interests, I think, if you're a bit more dynamic. And, but because of all the lesson preparations you've got to be hardworking, which I am.

Um … also, if you've got children, I think teaching's very good 'coz, you know, you can have holidays at the same time as the children.

Um … I also come from a family where there are a lot of teachers, so [y'know] it's carrying on a family tradition.

Oh, another, another thing, I think is that I'm very easily bored, and, um, you know, you, with teaching, you have different students every term, um, all sorts of different levels and you're never doing the same thing. I would hate to have to do the same thing year in, year out.

Ah, so, by chance I think I got the right job for my … for me. Um … I think when you are choosing a job, though, um, it's important to know yourself. Er, because, for example, if you decided you wanted to be an air hostess because it was really glamorous and exciting, er… but you yourself, er… weren't a very patient person, or, or, or rather shy, then you, you would be choosing an unrealistic job f… for yourself. So, yes, um, know yourself, that's the most important thing.

Unit 2, Lesson 2, Activity 2

Once, a few years ago, when I was a television reporter, I had to fly off suddenly to interview the Prime Minister. The office had booked a two-seater plane to get me there quickly, so I turned up at the airport and looked round impatiently for my pilot. There was nobody around except me and this blonde girl who also seemed to be waiting for someone. After a bout twenty minutes or so, I asked the blonde girl where the pilot might be, and if she knew the reason for the delay. As I started to speak to her, I realised the mistake, and so did she. 'Oh God,' she said to me. 'Are you the reporter?' I looked at her and said, 'Are you the pilot?' The answer was 'yes' to both questions! We had both assumed that because of the jobs, the people we were waiting for would be men! We all make judgements about people on the basis of what they look like, their clothes, their face and according to what sex they are, even though the truth is often very different. Do you make instant judgements about people? Do Activity 3 in your book and find out.

Unit 2, Lesson 3, Activities 1, 2 and 3

Counsellor: Hello, David.
David: Hello, er… Mrs Purkiss.
Counsellor: Right, now, first of all, what's your surname and how old are you?
David: My full name is David Macintosh and I'm 25.
Counsellor: And what qualifications have you got?
David: Er… I did 'A' levels at the local comprehensive, then I did a university degree in geography.
Counsellor: OK. How would you describe yourself, David?
David: Well, I suppose I'm quite good with people. Um … I like working with people anyway. I like a challenge, I'm patient, um… and practical… um…
Counsellor: Right. And what work have you done before?
David: Mostly temporary work since I graduated. Er, I haven't done anything related to geography at all. I was a postman for six months, er… a porter in a hospital, that was quite good, I liked working with the people there, and at the moment I'm working part-time in a library, er… but I've been looking for full-time work for over six months, and er… I'm not sure what career I want, which is why I've come here.
Counsellor: OK. What jobs are you interested in?
David: I'd really like to work outside. Er… maybe travel a bit. I speak French, so I'd like to use that too. Er… although I enjoyed my university degree, I think I'd like to do something different.
Counsellor: Have you thought about environmental work?
David: That would be interesting…
Counsellor: Let's have a look at the career card then. Well, it says here you have to have a university degree in either environmental science or geography – so that's OK for you – and you should apply in writing direct to one of the organizations on this list, or write for information about postgraduate courses. So you needn't have a specific qualification for that. One of the organizations on the list is looking for graduates with languages, too, so your French would be useful.
David: Yeah… that sounds excellent!
Counsellor: Also you should be between 23 and 35, in good health and you must be good at dealing with people because you'll have to work with other people.
David: Right… Yes… Well, um… the other career I've been thinking about is teaching. Er… what qualifications do I have to have for that?
Counsellor: Again, you must be good with people. It

depends on what kind of teaching you want to do. If you want to teach in state schools, you must have a teaching qualification – that's a one-year course. In some private schools you don't have to have a teaching qualification. But you should think carefully about teaching, because you must be very interested in your subject if you're going to teach it for a long time.
David: Yes, I suppose that's true. I would really like to do something related to geography, but… er… a bit wider. Maybe I should find out about the environmental work from one of the organizations you said earlier. Could I write the names down, please?
Counsellor: Yes, of course. You should send them a CV when you write. Is there any other career you'd like to discuss?
David: No, I think that's OK for now. Thank you very much for your help.

Unit 3, Lesson 1, Activities 6 and 7

Interviewer: With us is Imelda Topping who's a model and she's going to slip on a T-shirt now, a black T-shirt. It looks like a perfectly… well it's quite cool in here really, but we can already see a clear design coming out on your front. Ha… that must attract people's attention!
Imelda: Huh… yes! Er… the shape of a dolphin is beginning to appear. Er… it's red and brown.. um in the centre where it's the warmest part, it's going blue…
Interviewer: Imelda, would you go out, buy these clothes and wear them every day?
Imelda: Er… I think I would. Um … what I'd like to see is, say, some floral designs, where the flowers changed colour, that'd be pretty.
Interviewer: And where would you wear them?
Imelda: Oh, I'd wear them out in the evening, for example to discos, definitely. It would be really interesting to have something really different to wear, instead of the same things as everyone else.
Interviewer: The colours are still changing as we speak
Imelda: Ha, ha… Yes, some parts are going bright violet. Huh… I wouldn't like my hottest parts going bright violet…
Interviewer: Moira, you're the designer. Isn't that a major problem, that it's going to show up embarrassing bits, like under the arms?
Moira: Oh, it's possible, but, er… you can actually select the parts which you want to paint the ink on. On the other hand you can also focus on particular parts of the body if you want to – like Madonna would do, for example – and draw attention to them. For some people, that's a real advantage.
Interviewer: I've also heard that they change colour in the wash. Now, that would be a problem if you bought, say, blue, and then discovered you had a pink shirt, and it didn't suit you.
Moira: Well, the cheaper versions might do that, but you get what you pay for – most of them don't change like that.

Unit 3, Lesson 2, Activity 3

Interviewer: When Stuart Bexon was refused permission to build a house in a beautiful part of Britain, the Cotswolds, he refused to bury his dreams

and decided to bury his house instead. Good morning, Mr Bexon.
Stuart Bexon: Good morning.
Interviewer: Well, we're standing outside your front door now.
Stuart Bexon: Yes, would you like me to show you round?
Interviewer: Thanks. Ah… the house is egg-shaped, oval.
Stuart Bexon: That's right. Now, as… as you can see, in the middle there's er… a big open space which has the largest of the circular windows in the house. I use this as a day-room because it's so light. Then, in the point of the 'egg' is the er… observatory. You have a wonderful view of the sky, er… and I'm learning about the stars, in fact.
Interviewer: So you don't feel trapped under the ground?
Stuart Bexon: Oh, not at all! Well, there's plenty of light because each room has got a domed window. Oh… and I love my swimming pool. It's also useful because it helps to heat the rest of the house. Now, in the area to the right of the pool is my living room. Now, on the other side of the house, on the right of the entrance, is the kitchen, which has the garage leading off from it. And beyond the kitchen there's the dining room.
Interviewer: Oh, very romantic, being able to eat by moonlight!
Stuart Bexon: That's right. Now let's move on. Now diagonally opposite the dining room is the guest room. Immediately to the left of that is a bathroom and, to the right, a third bedroom. Again, it's convenient for visitors to be near their bathroom and not have to share with me. In fact, on either side of the side entrance there is a bathroom. However, this other one is an en suite bathroom. It's linked to my bedroom.
Interviewer: Oh yes, what a cosy room. I must say that the whole house feels comfortable. Doesn't it get cold?
Stuart Bexon: Oh, of course not! All the outer walls and floors are lined with a waterproof mixture.
Interviewer: Really!
Stuart Bexon: Yes. Er …we're … we're near the end now. Er … next to the entrance is my study. Now, it's tucked into this corner, by the entrance, the walls are very curved.
Interviewer: Yes. I've noticed the walls. Are there any straight walls in the house?
Stuart Bexon: No. Not one, except the garage, but that isn't really in the house.
Interviewer: Well, it's certainly a very interesting house. Thank you very much for showing me round.
Stuart Bexon: Well … that's quite alright.

Unit 3, Lesson 3, Activity 5

Man: Hello.
Lesley: Hello, I … I'm Lesley, I phoned you earlier about the computer.
Man: Oh yes, come through, it's just in here.
Lesley: Oh … I thought it was nearly new, it looks quite old.
Man: Oh, yes, don't worry, that's because it's dark in here. Um …, hold on, I'll, I'll put the light on.
Lesley: Hmm. How old did you say it was?
Man: Ah, well, my wife put the advert in the paper. She said it was four months old. It's actually a bit

older than that …

Lesley: Yes, it looks about four years old. Er … what are these marks on the side?

Man: Um … that's where it, er, well, fell off the desk. … ha … but it's only a low desk, I mean, nothing was damaged, really.

Lesley: So it's not really in 'excellent condition' like you said in the advert, is it?

Man: Ha, ha, ha …

Lesley: I see it has twin drives …

Man: Yes, all working perfectly

Lesley: And a light pen.

Man: Yes, that's right.

Lesley: Can I see it working?

Man: Of course. Um … I'll, I'll just plug it in. Um … ha, ha, I'm afraid it can be a bit difficult sometimes … Right, there we are!

Lesley: Well, the screen is a bit dim … Oh! it's gone off!

Man: Oh, you just have to move the wire a bit …

Lesley: Look, Mr, um … Evans, er … I really don't think you've been very honest here. It's obviously not in very good condition – in fact it doesn't seem to work at all. I would hardly describe it as a bargain, and I certainly think £450 is much too expensive. I'll be going now.

Man: But, look, it … it's working now …

Unit 4, Lesson 1, Activities 4 and 5

1

It's, er … actually very safe, but what's great about it is that it feels dangerous and when you stand on the edge and look down and let go … wow! I like it because I don't need any training or equipment. Er … you're lifted about 50 metres up by a specially built jump station and you're held by three ropes, not one. Er … when you're falling you … you travel at over 70 kilometres an hour, but it's … it's like a car braking gently when you slow down. Then you bounce back up to 30 metres. You never touch the ground. You feel fantastic afterwards. I've jumped off bridges mostly. It's quite expensive I suppose, but it's worth it – about £25 every jump.

2

We decided to go on the trip because a friend of mine bought the latest magazine about the game to school. Sometimes it can be quite expensive, but you play on about 50 hectares, so I guess it has to be. Costs £15 for the day, and 4 pence for each ball, which isn't bad. I went in a group of about twenty people, which is the maximum number allowed, and we had to set off very early in the morning. When we arrived the marshals took us to the playing area. Marshals go round and see who has been hit and who hasn't. They gave us all the equipment, goggles, guns, gas, everything like that, and then they gave us a safety training talk. That's really important. You divide off into two groups and you each have a home base and a flag. The idea is to capture the enemy flag and take it back to your own base. You can shoot the others with your guns to stop 'em. When I played, I got shot in the first ten minutes of the game, which meant I had to stop playing, but I didn't mind, because it was so exhilarating. It's the most exciting game I've played.

3

Well, I first tried this because I live in the mountains and for the last few years there hasn't been enough snow to ski, so we've all tried different sports. You do need to be able to use diving equipment, though. I took a course in the local swimming pool first, and then had to get used to hitting the ball through water. You use an ordinary racquet, but the ball is weighted so it will stay under the water. Everything happens slowly, but I like it because it's really good exercise. When you move underwater you are pushing against the water which takes a lot of energy. But more than that it's a good laugh and it's not expensive. Also you can play in pairs, or in large groups, it doesn't matter. You have to buy the diving equipment, which can cost hundreds of pounds, or you can hire it for about £15 a day, but otherwise it's free. We play mainly in a local lake, although some people play in a deep swimming pool.

Unit 4, Lesson 2, Activity 3

1

Interviewer: Can you tell me your name, age, and how often you come here?

Philip: Er, my name is Philip McDonald, I'm 25 years of age and er … I come here pretty often 'coz I got nothing else to do really. I suppose the main reason would be boredom, um, second to that would be, well, I suppose I want to try my luck.

Interviewer: And, er, where do you get the money from?

Philip: I'm a self-employed graphic designer.

2

Interviewer: Can you tell me your name, age, and how often you come here?

Jane: Well, my name is Jane and I come here about, um, well almost every day really. Oh, and I'm 16. I usually come here after school, on the way home with my friends. It's on the way back, we walk past here on the way back.

Interviewer: Do you play the video games or the fruit machines?

Jane: You're not really supposed to play the fruit machines, you have to be 18. Sometimes we do, but I like the video games more, more exciting, you know, you're guaranteed to lose on the fruit machines, they're gambling, more for gambling really. It's more fun on the video games.

Interviewer: And where do you get the money from to play?

Jane: Well, I – some of my friends get pocket money from their parents. I don't, but I do a paper round on a Thursday, get a bit of cash from there, and I spend that mostly, not all of it, but quite a lot (laugh). Sometimes my mum gives me a bit extra if I'm short of cash.

3

Interviewer: Can you tell me your name, age, and why – er … how often you come here?

Paul: My name's Paul Warwick, I'm 17 and I come here, I don't know, maybe once a week, every two weeks, or so.

Interviewer: Do you come to play the fruit machines, or the video games?

Paul: Oh, I never play the fruit machines, you're on to a loser there. I just play the video games. Some of my mates come here quite often, they play the fruit machines, but they always lose. It's not worth it. The video games in this arcade are quite good, so that's what I do.

Interviewer: Now, where do you get the money from?

Paul: I do a Saturday job.

4

Interviewer: Can you tell me your name, age, and how often you come here?

Alistair: My name's Alistair, I'm 19 and I come here a couple of times a week, sometimes more, depends on how bored I am. I'm a student and it's nice to come here to relax, 'specially if I'm doing exams or something, bit of escapism I guess, ha, I don't know.

Interviewer: And where do you get the money from to play,

if you're a student?

Alistair: Well, I use money from my grant. Um … sometimes I do the odd night in a pub or help out my mate who's got a – a stall on the market, and earn a bit there. You don't get much on a grant these days.

Interviewer: Do you ever win much?

Alistair: Oh, I don't really play the fruit machines that often. It's more the video games. I only play the fruit machines if I've been watching someone else who hasn't, you know, won anything. Then if you go up after them you can clean up.

Unit 4, Lesson 3, Activity 1

1: Where is the smallest bone in your body?

2: How many teeth should a healthy adult have?

3: What's the most common word in the English language?

4: Spell accommodation.

5: What's the name of the mountain which is the most photographed, painted and climbed in the world?

6: What does a meteorologist study?

7: Which is the world's most spoken language?

8: Who, on average, live longer? Men or women?

Unit 5, Lesson 1, Activity 9

'Oh no!' Mrs Crisp cried in horror. 'Was my husband really afraid of having his tooth out? Did he start to panic? Did he jump out of the window?' Mrs Crisp looked very upset. She stood in the doorway staring at the window, then at the dentist again, then at the window. 'What happened, what happened?' She looked all round the room, but couldn't see Mr Crisp anywhere. The room looked like any normal dentist's surgery. A large chair, lots of white cupboards, and lots of horrible metal instruments.

'I was washing my hands outside when it happened,' replied the dentist finally, wiping his forehead with a handkerchief. He sank into his chair, looking exhausted. 'When I came in, the nurse was in the room, and everything looked the same as it had done before, well, much the same as it does now, in fact. Well, I looked over at the window and saw his legs, er … that is, your husband's legs, Mrs Crisp, and they were disappearing over the edge. His legs looked all right, Mrs Crisp, but I'm afraid that's all I could see … '

Mrs Crisp hurried over to the window and looked down. The ground was only about one metre below, and it looked quite soft. But there was no sign of her husband at all. She looked to the right and left: there were a couple of trees, some flowers, then the car park. The Crisps' car was still parked where they had left it. Mrs Crisp turned back to the dentist …

Unit 5, Lesson 2, Activity 3

'I … I've been on the telephone,' the dentist explained. 'There's a rescue helicopter searching for him right now. I've also been in contact with the Weather Office to find out about wind direction and wind speed, so maybe we can guess where he is.' The phone rang and the dentist quickly grabbed the receiver. After a short conversation he replaced the phone and looked hard at Mrs Crisp. 'Are you and your husband planning to have a holiday in Europe soon?' he asked. 'No, we are not,' Mrs Crisp said, shaking her head. 'Oh … that's a pity,' replied the dentist, 'because the Weather man isn't sure, but he thinks the wind might blow your husband over the Channel into France! You could have joined him there and you'd only have to pay one fare!'

The phone rang loudly again. It was the newsroom. A British Airways passenger jet had almost hit a pedestrian just after it had taken off. 'I think we might have found him at last,' cried the dentist excitedly. 'And he's in good shape, too. Apparently he shook his fist and swore at the pilot.'

Mrs Crisp started to feel happier and look a little more cheerful at this news. The nurse came in, but she was still so pale that the dentist decided to close the surgery, and went out to tell the rest of his patients that all the other appointments had been cancelled. Then he took the nurse and Mrs Crisp into his back room, where they all had a cup of tea.

The phone on the dentist's desk rang yet again, and he hurried out to answer it. Minutes later, he returned, obviously excited, and said: 'Guess who I've been talking to? Your husband! He told me that apart from the problem with the aeroplane, he quite enjoyed the flight. After a while he discovered that he could go down if he burped. He floated over a nudist camp in the South of England, and he told me that he wanted to land there, but he missed it because he had to say 'excuse me' after every burp, so he didn't have time. Anyway, he came down on some telephone wires, not far away, and that's when a farmer helped him down and took him to the nearest telephone box.'

Unit 5, Lesson 3, Activity 4

Mrs Crisp was still angry. It wasn't just that she was worried, it was the fact that Mr Crisp had been so interested in the nudist camp. He asked the dentist to give him the name of the gas so he could have some more! He told him that he wanted to go to the South of France without her! He said that he had had a nice flight! All the time she had been worried sick.

She was still angry when her husband arrived home. The dentist told her that he would be unconscious for a while, and it was true – two ambulance men carried him into the house on a stretcher, but she didn't feel sorry for him. Even when he started to wake up slowly, she didn't feel sorry for him. She went out and made a cup of hot, strong tea.

'Are you awake yet?' she asked him. He started to speak, but before the words were out of his mouth,

she poured the hot tea over his head. 'Well, this will wake you up!' she shouted. Mr Crisp jumped up and ran for the door. 'Ww … what are you doing?' he cried. 'Ww … what's happening?'

'Ah, ho, ho, … Ah, ha, ha … I see you're feeling much better already,' Mrs Crisp laughed, as she picked up the cup and saucer.

Mr Crisp ran out of the house, closely followed by two flying saucers.

[WHOLE STORY]

The small, wrinkled woman sitting in the corner of the dentist's waiting room had been fidgeting for some time. First, she got up and walked around. After that she whistled, and hummed to herself. Meanwhile, the four other occupants of the room sat quietly, looking at her as the minutes ticked by. Suddenly, she looked round at the four other occupants in the room and burst out: 'Could I go in next? I'm sure something's happened to my husband. He's been in there for absolutely ages!'

'Certainly,' said the next patient very quickly, with a look of relief on his face. Without further ado, Mrs Crisp walked boldly into the dentist's surgery. The dentist, at his desk, was just replacing his phone. He looked up as she walked in and said: 'Er … you must be Mrs Crisp, the wife of my patient.'

'Yes,' she replied angrily. 'Where is he? He's been in here for such a long time.'

When she said this the dentist looked embarrassed and drummed his fingers on the desk. 'Um... there's been a mishap. Nothing serious. You see the open window there...' and he pointed to the wide open window next to the dentist's chair.

'Oh no!' Mrs Crisp cried in horror. 'Was my husband really afraid of having his tooth out? Did he start to panic? Did he jump out of the window?' Mrs Crisp looked very upset. She stood in the doorway staring at the window, then at the dentist again, then at the window. 'What happened? What happened?' She looked all round the room but couldn't see Mr Crisp anywhere. The room looked like any normal dentist's surgery. A large chair, lots of white cupboards, and lots of horrible metal instruments.

'I was washing my hands outside when it happened,' replied the dentist, finally, wiping his forehead with a handkerchief. He sank into his chair, looking exhausted. 'When I came in, the nurse was in the room and everything looked the same as it had done before, well, much the same as it does now, in fact. Well, I looked over at the window and saw his legs, er … that is your husband's legs, Mrs Crisp, and they were disappearing over the edge. His legs looked all right, Mrs Crisp, but I'm afraid that's all I could see...'

Mrs Crisp hurried over to the window and looked down. The ground was only about one metre below, and it looked quite soft. But there was no sign of her husband at all. She looked to the right and left: there were a couple of trees, some flowers, then the car park. The Crisps' car was still parked where they had left it. Mrs Crisp turned back to the dentist.

'He couldn't have hurt himself if he had thrown himself out,' she said, puzzled. 'Where is he?'

'He didn't go down, ' said the dentist, 'he went up!'

'Ww … what do you mean, up?'

'Well, he wanted to have gas and we had to use a new cylinder. But it must have been the wrong type of gas. As he was breathing it in, the nurse said he became very light and she had to hold him down in the chair. Then she smelt the gas herself and it smelt so strange that she let go of your husband. The window was open and he floated out. It gave her such a shock she

screamed. That's when I ran in, when I heard her, and as I rushed in, she fainted.'

Mrs Crisp was frantic. 'I'm not worried about her... What about my husband!'

'I … I've been on the telephone,' the dentist explained. 'There's a rescue helicopter searching for him right now. I've also been in contact with the Weather Office to find out about wind direction and wind speed, so maybe we can guess where he is.' The phone rang and the dentist quickly grabbed the receiver. After a short conversation he replaced the phone and looked hard at Mrs Crisp. 'Are you and your husband planning to have a holiday in Europe soon?' he asked. 'No, we are not,' Mrs Crisp said, shaking her head. 'Oh … that's a pity,' replied the dentist, 'because the Weather man isn't sure, but he thinks the wind might blow your husband over the Channel into France! You could have joined him there and you'd only have to pay one fare!'

The phone rang loudly again. It was the newsroom. A British Airways passenger jet had almost hit a pedestrian just after it had taken off. 'I think we might have found him at last,' cried the dentist excitedly. 'And he's in good shape, too. Apparently he shook his fist and swore at the pilot.'

Mrs Crisp started to feel happier and look a little more cheerful at this news. The nurse came in, but she was still so pale that the dentist decided to close the surgery, and went out to tell the rest of his patients that all the other appointments had been cancelled. Then he took the nurse and Mrs Crisp into his back room where they all had a cup of tea.

The phone on the dentist's desk rang yet again, and he hurried out to answer it. Minutes later, he returned, obviously excited, and said: 'Guess who I've been talking to? Your husband! He told me that apart from the problem with the aeroplane, he quite enjoyed the flight. After a while he discovered that he could go down if he burped. He floated over a nudist camp in the South of England, and he told me that he wanted to land there, but he missed it because he had to say 'excuse me' after every burp, so he didn't have time. Anyway, he came down on some telephone wires not far away, and that's when a farmer helped him down and took him to the nearest telephone box.'

'That's when he rang me,' the dentist said. 'He asked me what the name of the gas I used was so that he can refuel and take off again to Nice and the Riviera in the South of France. He also asked me if you were here. I told him you were and he put the phone down immediately.'

'He did, did he?' said Mrs Crisp, grinding her teeth angrily.

The dentist looked at her sympathetically.

'I gave him the name of the gas he should have had. When he takes that it'll knock him out. The local dentist will then arrange for Mr Crisp to be transported home.'

Mrs Crisp was not happy. 'He'll wish he was still unconscious when I get hold of him,' she muttered grimly as she left.

Mrs Crisp was still angry. It wasn't just that she was worried, it was the fact that Mr Crisp had been so interested in the nudist camp. He asked the dentist to give him the name of the gas, so he could have some more! He told him that he wanted to go to the South of France without her! He said that he had had a nice flight! All the time she had been worried sick.

She was still angry when her husband arrived home. The dentist told her that he would be unconscious for a while, and it was true – two ambulance men carried him into the house on a stretcher, but she didn't feel sorry for him. Even when he started to wake up slowly, she didn't feel sorry for him. She went out and made a cup of hot, strong tea.

'Are you awake yet?' she asked him. He started to speak, but before the words were out of his mouth, she poured the hot tea over his head. 'Well, this will wake you up!' she shouted. Mr Crisp jumped up and ran for the door. 'Ww … what are you doing?' he cried. 'Ww … what's happening?'

'Ah, ho, ho … Ah, ha, ha … I see you're feeling much better already,' Mrs Crisp laughed, as she picked up the cup and saucer.

Mr Crisp ran out of the house, closely followed by two flying saucers.

Unit 6, Lesson 1, Activities 3 and 4

Announcer: Good morning. Today, in our series following the various jobs involved in crime prevention, we're looking at the Customs Service. If you thought it was just a question of stopping and searching people going through the green channel, you'd be wrong, as our reporter, Lesley Amis, found out last week when she spent a day with customs officials and staff at London's third airport at Stansted.

Reporter: It's half past ten in the morning and I'm standing in the baggage handling area of Stansted Airport, just 40 minutes away from the heart of London. In front of me now is Andrew McGowen, watching closely as an excited black and white spaniel scrambles across a row of assorted bags, suitcases and holdalls, all waiting to go down the conveyor belt into the baggage claim area. Andrew, what exactly are you watching out for here?

Andrew: Well, you have to watch out for the signs from the dog, any biting, clawing, scratching, barking. It's up to you as the handler to read that little extra bit of body language. It might be food, this dog's very good at finding food! Or it might be something more interesting. Looks like he's a bit keen on that bag there. Let's go and have a look at that.

Reporter: Andrew's opening the bag now and sorting through. He's looking for anything which will give any indications that the owner of the luggage is a drugs user. He's taken out a couple of pairs of jeans and is searching the pockets.

Andrew: He's obviously a scuba diver. He's off a flight from Barbados, must've gone there for the diving. I don't think there'll be anything in this one. Probably looks after his health, so is less likely to be a user. Back to the other bags.

Reporter: Well, we're in the customs hall now and I'm with another officer here, Jim Cullon. Jim, what are you watching out for here?

Jim: Er, well, Baron, that's one of the dogs, got excited about a grey suitcase. Um … we put a marker bag next to it and one of the officers in the baggage reclaim has spotted the owner so we're waiting for him up here. Ah, this looks like him now.

Reporter: He's an average-looking man of about 26 or 28. Jim's pulling him over now and asking him some questions. Another officer is searching his bag and it looks like he's found something. He's pulling out a small bag. Yes … it looks like they're cautioning him, they're picking up the bag and taking him off into the interrogation room. Jim's coming back out

now. Jim, any news?

Jim: Well, we've found a small amount of what looks like marijuana. He's come off a flight from Amsterdam, it's legal there to carry small quantities of marijuana. He may have more on him, er … he'll be thoroughly searched now, but we don't think he'll have any more. He probably won't be prosecuted for such a small amount.

Unit 6, Lesson 3, Activities 2 and 3

Woman: Hey, have you read the paper yet? Look here, it says that a man has stolen some toys from that big department store in town.

Man: No, I haven't read that bit yet. What's happened?

Woman: Well, his name's Mark Thompson. Apparently the store manager caught him shoplifting just before Christmas.

Man: Um … what's happened to him, then? Has he been put in prison?

Woman: Well it says here in this week's paper that he's got to go to a different court for them to decide what to do with him. Apparently, he's been unemployed for over 18 months, and he said he felt sorry for his children because he couldn't buy them any Christmas presents.

Man: Well, that's no excuse. I mean, I can understand, but there're a lot of people who are unemployed and they don't all go around stealing.

Woman: Yes, that's true. But you can see how he would have felt, seeing all those toys in that huge store, just before Christmas. It says here he's been into the store several times and has offered to pay for the toys.

Man: What did they say about that?

Woman: Well, the store manager won't accept that. It's their policy to prosecute, apparently.

Man: Well, I think he should go to prison. Not for very long, maybe a short sentence.

Woman: But if he's in prison, he can't look for a job, and he might do the same thing again.

Man: Uh, perhaps they should give him a fine. Maybe £50 or something and a suspended sentence.

Woman: I think the store manager should let him pay for the toys and maybe he should be put on probation.

Unit 6, Lesson 3, Activity 4

Man: Well, I think he should go to prison. Not for very long, maybe a short sentence.

Woman: But if he's in prison, he can't look for a job, and he might do the same thing again.

Man: Uh, perhaps they should give him a fine. Maybe £50 or something and a suspended sentence.

Woman: I think the store manager should let him pay for the toys and maybe he should be put on probation.

Unit 7, Lesson 1, Activity 7

People do say I'm strange-looking and mysterious, but I don't mind. I think it's a bit of a compliment, actually. Other children at school used to say that all the time. Things like 'Let's get the curly-headed

strange one.' I don't like children. My brother Adam is the same as me. He doesn't have any friends of his own age, either.

I retired from school a year ago because all we were doing was kicking a ball around. To me that's not logical. I have a good mind, and like to use it. I enjoy my business, I don't like playing. I go swimming for exercise, I think that's enough sport.

I'm old fashioned, I suppose. I like correct behaviour. I don't like jeans and scruffy clothes, I like to look neat and tidy. I've dressed in suits and ties ever since I was six years old.

I don't have many hobbies really, because I spend most of my time at the flower shop or doing my school work. But in the evenings I like to do embroidery, sewing pictures onto cushions and that sort of thing. It's nice to spend the evening with my sewing and my family. It's very relaxing. We don't watch television at home. We sit and talk as a family, we're very close.

My mother says I'm stingy with money and that I never spend any. I suppose that's true, but I need to save because I need to be rich in the future. I have a plan for my life and I will need a lot of money to do it. You see, I am going to be the youngest ever Member of Parliament, and then I'm going to be prime minister. I will be a much better prime minister than Mrs Thatcher or John Major. As soon as I get better at mathematics I will make an exact plan of what I'm going to do when I'm in charge.

Unit 7, Lesson 2, Activities 6 and 7

Interviewer: So tell me, Mr Harvey, you're an expert in the field of child care, what do you think of this so-called diet and fitness programme of Marv Marinovich's?

Expert: Well, Lesley, this is one of the biggest problems facing kids these days. You see, statisticians in the US show that, yes, a lot of kids in the US are more unhealthy than in the past, and some are dangerously fat. But you know these sporty superkids, (and Marinovich isn't the only father doing this,) these kids are frankly damaging their bodies with unnatural stresses and strains.

Interviewer: So you're saying it's dangerous?

Expert: Yes, that's right. You see, repetitive overuse of certain muscles or body parts can be damaging in adults, as we all know, but in children it's even worse, and can be permanent. Marinovich says that the programme he's developed for Mikhail is different, and he says that it will enable Mikhail to become a very successful athlete. But you know, often what happens with these kids is that they become the unhappy toy. The hardest thing to accept often, is that it is the parents who are making decisions that the kids are not allowed to have any opinion about. The kids are then under a lot of psychological pressure.

Interviewer: Do you think this is what has happened to Todd?

Expert: Yes, I do. Todd's nickname is Robo-quarterback, and like Robocop, he just goes on and on and on playing, blindly. He plays for the Los Angeles Raiders and, at 21, he's a millionaire. Now, that's great, but being a celebrity is hard, and Todd himself has admitted that. The real tragedy is that he has been forced to live an unnatural life very different from normal children. And if his career ends suddenly, from an injury for example, he could be left with nothing, as he's had absolutely no other training. That's frightening for him.

Unit 7, Lesson 3, Activities 3 and 4

The problem with these young sportsmen and women is that the sport takes over their whole life. Hana Mandlikova said in 1981, when she was just nineteen, that she felt she wasn't living, she was only a machine practising and playing, practising and playing. Tennis, you see, has changed. It's no longer a game for women and men, but for young girls and boys, and in tennis it seems especially for young girls, Hana, for example, Tracy Austin, of course, and Jennifer Capriati, who was only fourteen when she became the youngest seed to play at Wimbledon.

But, you see, although it's very exciting to be so young and successful, there are also casualties: Tracy Austin at sixteen had already won the US Open Championship and was the world's Number 2. Everything seemed wonderful, then she had a stress fracture in her back and had to leave the game before she was 21. She's a tennis commentator for American TV now, and is happy, but when she was young, she didn't have any friends outside tennis, much like Hana. All she concentrated on was practising and playing, and not what most young girls spend their time doing.

Jennifer Capriati also suffered. When she was fifteen she used to have terrible arguments with her parents over school work, which she never had time for. Now she has bigger problems, as we've read in the papers recently about shoplifting.

Parents are often a problem, because they want the child to succeed because they haven't succeeded in something in their lives, or because they want their children to make lots of money for them. In other cases, the child comes to rely very heavily on family. Monica Seles, who was only thirteen when the family moved from Yugoslavia to the United States, relies completely on her mother, father and brother, which is very nice, but not very natural.

Hana Mandlikova is one of the saddest victims of this. She was always very lonely, and got married when she was only 24, but the marriage only lasted two years, and she blames tennis for the problems she had.

The worrying thing is that there seems to be no lower age limit these days. Nick Bollettieri, a top trainer, has apparently found a ten-year-old Russian to coach. I'm worried that we'll end up having a tennis champion who is worth millions of dollars and still in nappies!

Unit 7, Lesson 3, Activity 5

The best advice I can give to young people hoping to have a successful sporting career is to say work hard and play hard, because a balanced personality helps you to cope with the pressures of a sporting career. Nobody should concentrate on just one area and cut everything else out. If you do, and anything goes wrong, you have nothing else in your life. So it's a good idea to make time to meet friends, and it's important to know how to get on well with people. As far as parents go, I don't think they should interfere in their child's life, especially not if it's just a question of money. Parents ought to think very carefully about their reasons for encouraging their children and make sure it is what the child wants. That's the most important thing.

Unit 8, Lesson 1, Activities 1 and 2

Jane Leary: Hello, I'm Jane Leary and welcome to our regular phone-in slot concerning today's topical issues. Today we have Doctor Malcolm Jeffries with us in the studio to answer your questions about acupuncture, an alternative healing technique used by many to combat anything from smoking to skin problems. Good morning, Dr Jeffries.

Doctor Jeffries: Good morning, Jane.

Jane Leary: Before we open the phone lines, can you tell us a little bit about the technique? Um, firstly, how does it work?

Doctor Jeffries: Well, when you're healthy there is a free flow of energy through the body; this is called Chi, and when you're sick, there's a block in this flow of energy. Acupuncture tries to unblock this flow by putting needles into specific places according to the illness.

Jane Leary: I see. And, um, who exactly can it help?

Doctor Jeffries: Well, no one can predict who will respond to acupuncture but anything up to 70 per cent of those suffering from stress, backache and insomnia find it helpful. It also helps people who want to lose weight and give up smoking, for example.

Jane Leary: Mmm, and what are the needles like, exactly?

Doctor Jeffries: Well, everybody has the same sort of needles, it doesn't matter if the person is fat or thin, young or old. One to twenty needles are used at a time, if they are to go in your hand or head, they're fairly short, about fifteen millimetres long, and if they're going elsewhere they're longer, about 3 centimetres. But don't worry, there's no pain and there's rarely any bleeding.

Jane Leary: Right, OK then, well, I think we can probably open the phone lines now. Could we have our first caller please? Hello, have you got a question for Dr Jeffries?

Unit 8, Lesson 2, Activities 4 and 5

I became a vegetarian about six years ago. Before that I had always eaten meat. Then I went on holiday to South America, and I stayed with a friend's family there. I'd met Susana, my friend, the year before when I was working at a language school and we'd got on really well, so she'd invited me to stay in Argentina with her family. They were really lovely, very welcoming and kind, and showed me all the attractions of the city and took me out every evening to a different restaurant. The only trouble was that meat, and especially beef, is a very traditional part of Argentinian meals and I ended up eating probably a whole cow during my two weeks there!

When I got back home my mother asked me if I'd had a good time, and I told her it had been wonderful. She'd prepared a special Sunday lunch for me to welcome me home, and I looked at the table and she had made roast beef! It was then that I decided to stop eating meat. I just couldn't eat it.

Lots of people give up eating meat for very different reasons. Some for religious reasons, others because they don't like the way cows, sheep, pigs and chickens are farmed, and I must say I have to agree with this, and some, like me, because I decided one day that I'd eaten enough meat in my life.

I feel much healthier now: after my holiday in Argentina, I had a lot of spots which I'd never had before, and I didn't really feel very well. I felt like my body was trying to tell me something. Since I've been eating vegetarian food my skin is a lot clearer. I don't get colds and sore throats as often as I used to do, either.

Some people think vegetarians are strange. One man, after I'd told him that I didn't eat meat actually had an argument with me about it! Other people think that not eating meat must be very boring, or very difficult, but I disagree: I think vegetarian food is much more exciting and varied. But mostly people accept it. I think it's something like five per cent of the population in Britain now that are vegetarian, so I'm not on my own!

Unit 8, Lesson 3, Activity 1

Close your eyes and relax. … Make sure you're comfortable … and think about your breathing. … Breathe gently in … and out … in … and out. … As you breathe in, let go of any tensions or worries. … Relax. … And now, feeling relaxed, in your imagination, go to a place that is special to you, … somewhere where you feel happy. … What is the place like? … Look around you and notice if there are any plants or people or animals. … How do you feel? … What are you wearing? … Are there any sounds in this place? … Think about why this place is special to you. … Now choose something from this special place to bring back to the classroom. … Take the thing. … And it's time to come back to the classroom. … Slowly … When I count to three you will open your eyes and remember everything that happened in your special place, and you will imagine the thing which you chose to bring back with you. … One … two … three …

Unit 8, Lesson 3, Activities 4 and 5

Interviewer: Matthew, I hear you have special powers, or gifts. Can you tell me when you first noticed them?

Matthew: Well, I was born in 1955 and I had a normal childhood until I was about eleven years old. Er … one night my father went downstairs into the living room and discovered a silver cup in the middle of the floor. We normally kept it in the cupboard. He called the family down but nobody could explain it, we were all astounded.

Interviewer: So what happened then?

Matthew: We sort of forgot about it for a couple of days, then four days later the same thing happened again, only more things were in the wrong place. My father thought it was a poltergeist, so contacted Dr Owen, a psychic investigator, who said that it wasn't a poltergeist, but me!

Interviewer: That must have been a bit worrying?

Matthew: Yes, it was. But then nothing happened for a while, until I was about fifteen. One night during the holidays from school I was reading in bed when suddenly the bed, along with me on it, flung itself into the middle of the room. I was terrified. I spent all night in my parents' room. The next morning the dining room looked like a bomb had hit it, things everywhere. Then lights starting turning themselves on and off, strange writing appeared on the walls, and sometimes, as we watched, we saw objects thrown up the stairs.

Interviewer: Did this only happen at home?

Matthew: No. Er … when I went back to school after the holiday – I was at boarding school, the first night the same thing happened with my bed, and also three other boys' beds did the same thing. A lot of them were frightened, but some of them thought it was funny.

Interviewer: Did you try to do anything to control these things?

Matthew: Yes, but then the automatic writing started. One day I was trying to write an essay and suddenly my hand dropped onto the paper and started writing without me even thinking. What I wrote wasn't even English. I was incredibly puzzled by it, but then it started happening a lot, sometimes in Russian, other times Latin, even Arabic. These are languages I've never learnt!

Interviewer: So, what connects all this to your healing powers?

Matthew: When I was eighteen I went to Canada, to see some scientists there who thought they could help me. I didn't like all the research, so I left and went to India.

Er … while I was travelling there I had what I can only describe as a mystical experience, I suddenly felt a lot of love and serenity, and I realised I could help sick people to get well. It made me very excited, and, er … that's when I decided to become a healer.

Unit 9, Lesson 1, Activities 2 and 3

My poor mother didn't know she was going to have twins. She had saved up to buy a lovely big pram for one, you see. My sister Diana was born and the doctor started to walk off, when suddenly I popped out! It was a real shock, especially as I was so small, and cried all the time.

We're identical twins and, although we dress differently now, we were always dressed in the same clothes as children, and often my mother even had a dress made out of the same material, which I think is awful.

Also, we were very quiet and shy, but because we were identical, we were always chosen to present the flowers to visitors at the school. Once we had to be pageboys in the school play and I absolutely hated it, and so did Diana. It was terrible, it really was.

In fact, I think that's one reason why we aren't very close now. We were treated as one person when we were young and I suppose we rebelled against it. For example, most people didn't even bother to learn our names, they just called us 'twin'. The first time people actually used my name was when I was eighteen and went away to college.

At school we did the same subjects and got similar marks. I remember we both won prizes once and they gave us the same book, which seemed silly to me because it would have been more useful to have two different books. We were very jealous of each other, though, so maybe it was better to give us the same thing.

People believed we should be together for everything, but I think they were wrong. We made each other worse, not better. One of the first times we went to the dentist, he asked us who was going first. Diana said she needed to go to the toilet, so I said I wanted to go as well. Before long we were both screaming and my mother had to take us home. She was really embarrassed!

Now we both have similar jobs, and our children say our voices are very similar and that we have the same mannerisms and things, but we don't really see each other very often.

Unit 9, Lesson 1, Activity 6

The twins were born in Llanelli in Wales in 1932. They both carry copies of a photograph taken about a year after that; they have studied it for hours, but they can't tell themselves apart, and nor can their mother! They had a very happy childhood, and were very close to their parents. The brothers did equally well at school, except during one term of woodwork when Keith made a jewellery box but Clive couldn't. They're still very puzzled about this because in everything else they were exactly the same.

In 1947 the twins left school to work together managing hotels in Bournemouth and in the Lake District, which they did until 1950, when they were conscripted into the army. When they left the army two years later, they signed up for the merchant navy. Because they had always got on so well together, they wanted to be on the same ship, but they discovered that brothers weren't allowed to work together on one ship. Keith tried to get special permission, but they refused, so both the twins went to work on different ships. Keith didn't like that and neither did Clive.

One day when they were on holiday in 1958, they went to London. They were walking down a street and noticed a woman trying to open a window. The twins went to help her. They found out her name was Georgia, and the three became friends. It was Clive who eventually married Georgia, on New Years Eve in 1958 and since then they have never been separated, Clive, Keith and Georgia. The three share a flat and socialise together.

Unlike with a lot of twins, the marriage hasn't caused any problems between the twins, there's no tension and the relationship is the same as it's always been. Clive says that there's absolutely no jealousy in their relationship, and that maybe that's the answer, life is not a competition for them.

Unit 9, Lesson 2, Activities 3 and 4

Boys will be boys

Look at little Peter, isn't he a terror
Shooting all the neighbours with his cowboy gun?
Screaming like a jet plane, always throwing something
I just can't control him. Trouble? He's a one.
Ah, but boys will be boys,
It's a fact of human nature,
And girls will grow up
To be mothers.
Look at little Janie, doesn't she look pretty?
Playing with her dolly, proper little mum.
Never being dirty, never being noisy,
Don't touch your sister, Peter, now look what you've

done!
Ah, but boys will be boys,
It's a fact of human nature,
And girls will grow up
To be mothers.

Unit 9, Lesson 2, Activity 5

Now what's come over Janie? Janie's turning nasty,
Left hook to the body, right hook to the eye.
Vicious little hussy, now Peter's started bawling,
What a bloody cissy! Who said you could cry?
Because boys must be boys,
It's a fact of human nature,
And girls must grow up
To be mothers.
Now the world's gone topsy-turvy, Janie wants a football
And Peter just seems happy pushing prams along.
It makes you feel so guilty, kids are such a worry,
Doctor, Doctor, tell me, where did we go wrong?
Because boys must be boys,
It's a fact of human nature,
And girls must grow up
To be mothers.
[Repeat whole of poem]

Unit 9, Lesson 2, Activity 8

1

Interviewer: Kerry, if you could live your life again, would you prefer to be a man or a woman?

Kerry: I'd definitely prefer to be a woman.

Interviewer: Why's that?

Kerry: Well, mainly because men can't have babies! I know it sounds stupid, but it's such a wonderful experience, and I wouldn't like to be deprived of it. Also, I think women are much more able to cope on their own than men, in a crisis or if there's a problem, a woman will work it out. Men seem to need someone, they can't cope on their own.

2

Interviewer: Rob, if you could live your life again, would you prefer to be a man or a woman?

Rob: Well, I think I'd like to try being a woman for a change.

Interviewer: Why's that?

Rob: Well, a couple of reasons for it, uh … I'd really like to kind of experience things from the other side. I've seen things as a man and I'd like to see what it's like to be a woman, a woman's feelings and reactions to things. Also how other people treat them, because I've spoken to a lot of women who've said that maybe they've been treated badly by men and by society in general, so I think it would be good for me to see things from the other side. And also I'm interested in how the psychology of women might be different from men. So I think for all those reasons it'd be nice to come back as a woman.

3

Interviewer: Paula, can you tell me, er … if you could live your life again, would you prefer to be a man or a woman?

Paula: Um … it's a difficult question, but I think I'd come back as a woman. The reason is that I don't like the way men hide their feelings. Er … they never cry, well, certainly in this culture, they can never say 'I love you'. On the other hand, I'd love to be able to come back for, say, 24 hours as a man. It would be wonderful to know what men really think and feel, out of curiosity more than anything.

4

Interviewer: Yves, if you could live your life again, would you prefer to be a man or a woman?

Yves: Um … I don't know, really, um as I'm a man I've no idea what it's like to be a woman, and I really can't say how I could answer that. I … let's put it this way, I've enjoyed being a man so in that respect I don't feel that I need to change it. Um … men think differently to women, they … everything's so different about them so I really wouldn't know. I've only been a man of course. Um … I think I'd like to be a man again.

Unit 9, Lesson 3, Activity 6

Well, the idea was to find out what life is like from the other side really. I was being sponsored and the money would go to cancer research. On that day the whole country was encouraged to be somebody else for the day. The first thing I found out was that most of the clothes in the men's shops were so unisex that they didn't make me look masculine. But finally, with a dark suit, a raincoat and a pair of heavy work boots, I looked OK. Then it was to the barber's. The barber only actually spoke to me once, when I tried to lean back for the shampoo. 'You're in a barber's now,' he said, pushing my face forwards over the sink, not back as they do in the hairdresser's, and then he cut my hair into a manly style, really short around the ears!

It was only when a make-up artist put on dark colour around my chin that I really started to look like a man. Then I asked a friend how I looked and er … he said my trousers were pulled too high. Unless I put my belt on my hips instead of my waist I wouldn't look aggressive. So I did that.

Unit 9, Lesson 3, Activity 7

Then I went out. As I was walking along I passed a street full of American cars, ambulances and policemen. I decided to try out my deep voice. 'What's going on?' I asked. 'It's the Vice President, sonny,' answered the policeman, hardly looking at me. And this was one of the main differences about being a man: all day on the streets nobody looked at me in the face. I have never felt so invisible.

I decided to try and get into a Men's Club, which didn't allow women to enter. Once I got through the doors and up the stairs there was no problem. I was treated wonderfully, everyone called me 'Sir', and the waiter brought me drinks without me even asking.

The next thing I did was go into a pub. Through the door I could see it was full of building workmen, so I nearly left. But then I realised they were making space for me near the bar, something which never happens if you are a woman.

At the end of the afternoon, all I could think about was a long, hot bath. I walked home the short way through the park. I would never do that in women's clothes. I was the same person, but as long as I wore men's clothes, people would treat me differently. Just to make sure I knew who I was, I stopped at the chemist to buy the brightest lipstick I could find!

Unit 10, Lesson 1, Activities 3 and 4

The Chinese name for Victoria Harbour is Fragrant Harbour er … referring to a perfume quality. However, today if you go to Hong Kong you see that Victoria Harbour is far from being a fragrant harbour, rather it is a polluted harbour. The reason for this is pollutants from factories around Hong Kong and more importantly the pollution from the huge population, over six million people live in Hong Kong and I believe two thirds live in the main city.

I myself have seen the harbour when it was quite brown and I wouldn't want to fall into it.

The rivers of Hong Kong are also polluted, polluted by farmers, er … for example, pig farmers who empty their waste into the rivers.

The question now is, what is Hong Kong going to do about this pollution? In recent years Hong Kong has become more environment-conscious. Um … the government is going to set up a new sewage plant and sewage is going to be treated before it is emptied into the harbour. However, this is not developing quickly because it is a non-profit-making business. People are more interested in what the government is going to do for tourism. They have said that they are going to spend money building a new airport which will be finished in a few years time …

Unit 10, Lesson 2, Activities 5 and 6

Stephanie: Well, what I found hard was stopping eating sweets at break-time, you know, chocolate. And also crisps. I used to bring crisps in, but the bags, the plastic, it's all rubbish which you can't just throw away 'coz it doesn't, you know, it stays and doesn't go away, ever. And also what we do is bring our lunch in a box now instead of plastic bags. My mum puts it in a box and I bring the same box every day. Not the same sandwiches, though. (laugh) It's good 'coz you don't waste things so much.

Alice: We've made some of the grounds of the school into a garden and we grow herbs and flowers and vegetables there like carrots and green beans and things. And onions. Another thing we do is we've started this project to help animals and wildlife, too. We've put these things up to feed the birds, and every day someone in the class has to make sure there is enough food for the birds. That's in the winter, though, because Mrs Evans says that birds can look after themselves in the summer. I like the birds.

Steven: We used to come to school in Dad's car every day, but now I come with three other friends. Our parents take it in turns to drive. My Dad says it's great because it's cheaper and he doesn't have to drive every day. Another thing that my Dad did was give up smoking 'coz it makes a lot of rubbish with the packets and the cigarette ends and ash, and also the smoke is bad for the ozone layer, our teacher told us, and anyway, my Dad wanted to give up and it gave him the excuse, I suppose.

Paul: Our teacher used to give us lots of photocopies for things like out of books and exercises that we used to do, but we decided that it wasn't a good idea because it uses a lot of paper and then there won't be any trees left. So we stopped. Now we use the books and if we need to we copy things into our exercise books. It's better in a way because when you copy it yourself you can learn it at the same time. Another thing the teachers do is now they use different pens for writing on the board. They have refills, you know, so that you can use them again, then you don't have to throw the pen away each time they run out.